Is _That_ in the Bible?

Fascinating Insights and Discoveries From the Book of Books

Ray Puen

Copyright © 2010 by Ray Puen
Third Edition

First Edition Copyright © 2008 by Ray Puen
Second Edition Copyright © 2008 by Ray Puen

Is That in the Bible?
by Ray Puen

Printed in the United States of America

ISBN 9781615797622

Scripture quotations are taken from the New King James Version. Copyright © 1991 by Thomas Nelson; and The New Living Translation. Copyright © 2004 by Tyndale House Publishers Inc.

www.xulonpress.com

Dedicated
To the glory of God

Foreword

Ray Puen and I have called each other friends for over a decade. People Stateside and abroad know this Christian author, evangelist, and Bible student for his quick wit and spirituality. Ray is the kind of guy who can make you laugh about yourself and bring you to tears over Christ in the blink of an eye. Serious as a heartbeat about the Bible, Ray really enjoys digging into God's Word. A book like this could only come from years of deep, passionate investigation of the Scriptures.

All of us at one time or another have come across parts of the Bible that left us muttering, "I wonder what that means?" Well, instead of leaving a trail of underlines, highlights, and question marks beside puzzling words, phrases, and verses in his study Bible, Ray has compiled an impressive lineup of catchy and challenging snippets from the Bible, researched and prayed over each one, and published them in this charming book. What's more, Ray's informal style – question-answer-Bible reference – makes it easy to check out anything he writes and come to your own biblical conclusions.

Ray might just as well have called this handy little volume, "What you always wanted to know about the Bible, but didn't know where to find it." Formatted for beginners, but packed with answers to many veteran questions, you'll want "Is _That_ in the Bible?" on hand when you study. With its crisp, context-cracking insights at your fingertips, you will capture the context of many unfamiliar passages, and understand others that have troubled you in the past.

As you use this book, I expect you to stop asking, "Is _that_ in the Bible?" and know it is. In fact, you will praise God that He enabled Ray to write it. Every lover of the Living and Written Word should have one in his or her library.

Lee J. Gugliotto, Ph.D.
Condon, Montana

Dr. Gugliotto is President of Empower Ministries and Bible Study Institute of Montana. The Evangelical Christian Publishers Association awarded him its prestigious Gold Medallion for *Handbook for Bible Study,* thereby honoring it as the international, interdenominational, Bible study book of 1996.

Acknowledgments

M aterial such as assembled in this collection isn't gener-
ated by deciding to write a book. It would result from
years of collecting nuggets from sermons, public lectures or
media. Unfortunately, I didn't keep a journal for this collection so that I could have included sources. I thus run some
risk by including items pried only from memory. I hope this
book elicits a response from any of the readership if anyone
recognizes where some of these sources might be. I would be
grateful to be so prompted that I may make corrections and
give proper credit in a later edition. (Email me at rpuen@
yahoo.com.)

Speaking of sources, my biggest challenge had to do with
entries that were best illumined by understanding Jewish
customs. Although I had started to collect these nuggets a
long time ago as a result of my online teaching experience,
the project received impetus from a seminary class I took
called Jewish Background of the Gospels. I was fascinated
by Jewish customs and how our understanding of scripture
can be immensely enriched by understanding cultural traditions and customs. I owe a debt of gratitude to my teacher of
that class, Prof. David Edery of The King's Seminary, who
not only inspired our class through his teaching but also read
the manuscript and provided valuable comments regarding
the Jewish customs I had chosen to write about. His insis-
tence on scholarship and citing of sources prevented me
from making unsupportable assumptions.

Dr. Lee Gugliotto also read the manuscript and recommended some corrections. I especially desired his input
because of his ministry that promotes and encourages
bible study, as evidenced in his teaching seminars and the

publication of his 1996 Gold Medallion-winning *Handbook for Bible Study.*

I wish I could say that the nuggets in this book were collected over a period of years in a scrapbook or some other more organized form. But I can't. I tried looking up possible sources to verify that there indeed was a lamp designed to have a handle curled around one's big toe from which has been proposed the explanation for the "lamp unto my feet and light unto my path." That's how I recalled the story I read in my youth, but memory cannot be the measurement by which to select any scripture nugget. So I had to leave that item out because I couldn't find any picture or mention of archaeological discovery of the lamp.

Because of my original online readership, I avoided using such terms as *theophany* (in explaining the term Angel of the Lord), or *anthropomorphic*, choosing instead to describe the word or term. I was aiming for the casual reader in my weekly distribution.

I treasure the many responses from online students who expressed their interest in being part of any continuing list after they were done with the course they had taken, in order to continue receiving the weekly quizzes. This convinced me that there was a wider spread of interest in God's word than I had suspected. I thank these many faceless respondents, none of whom I had the privilege of meeting when the book was being planned.

My wife Leni played a role in the formation of the daily quiz program that metamorphosed into this book. While recuperating from double hip replacement surgery, she spent the enforced inactivity in meditation on each day's One Year Bible reading, faithfully journaling her thoughts. We had a productive time discussing her written journal entries. When she asked if Tamar's twin sons by Judah were "replacement" for sons denied her from her two previous marriages, I said I didn't know (but I was fascinated to entertain her "Could it possibly be that…" type of probing). These questions started me on a casual search and inspired me to recommend the daily reading habit to my live and online classes.

I want to acknowledge the California house churches or leadership training groups in West Covina, Chino Hills, Loma Linda, Baldwin Park, Claremont, Eagle Rock, Fresno and Glendale on whom I tried some of these processes as encouragement to follow the Bible study plan and as teaching examples, both of hermeneutics (interpretation of scriptures) and of communicating the Word. The combined experience resulted in my being asked by my pastor to become the director of a Bible school at my church to nurture the members and equip them for small group ministry. I'm thankful for Pastor Ban Alsaybar's encouragement and would like to have been able to present him the first book. Unfortunately that opportunity forever slipped through my fingers earlier this year.

I'm grateful for the format of the One Year Bible that its publishers decided on. I'm convinced its scripture divisions were divinely inspired for the many instances we've discovered where a teaching principle in an Old Testament passage is mirrored in the New Testament reading for the same calendar day into which the passages are organized. Although I don't mind the difficult step of posting by email each following month's collection of scripture readings to the subscribers in the different countries participating in this never-ending year-round program, I look forward to the day when the One Year Bible will be published in Tamil, Hindi, Nepali, Thai, Swahili, and Tagalog – languages in the fields where we are active in house church planting. That's because the Basic Bible course that came out of this exercise is part of the training program overseas. To God be the glory for His Word in the One Year Bible format!

As I review the sequence of events that led to the publication of this book you are reading, I can't help but recognize how the Holy Spirit led at each step of the book's development. It was many times a moving experience for me as I paused to capture a particular insight from reading the Bible ahead of my classes in order to create the daily, then later weekly, quizzes. I fancy that many casual readers attracted by the title of the book or in cursory examination of any of its entries might be led to examine the original Book of books. I pray that this may be this collection's major contribution.

To God be the glory!

Preface

This book is the result of several free online classes I taught. Part of the discipline undergirding each of those classes was the daily Bible reading that is encouraged. In order to make the experience interesting rather than compulsory, I used the One Year Bible published by Tyndale House Publishers, Inc. and developed teaser questions from the daily reading to post to the students. I would then provide the answers the next day along with questions for the following day's reading. In time, I changed the frequency so that I posted the whole week's questions in advance and the answers the following week along with the new questions.

This approach proved so effective in encouraging people to form the daily Bible reading habit that I imported the experience into my weekly house church meetings. Even the book title came out of that experience as students would post "I-didn't-know-that-was-in-the-Bible!" responses. That experience polished the approach as I designed a quiz form on which the house church members would write down answers to only one question from the three daily study questions I had handed out the week before. By not knowing which daily question I would use, they had to look up the answers to all three. It turned to be a constructive experience.

When we integrated the same program overseas by email, I had to make an adjustment because the Nepal leaders gather together with the field workers only once a month. In this instance, I send the whole month's worth of study questions to their Overseer and he translates them into Nepali for distribution. Because the One Year Bible isn't available in Nepali, I would email the whole month's readings before their meetings. The leaders then would use the questions as part of the nurture portion of their house church meetings.

It is a joy to receive reports back of former Hindus in various house churches responding to Bible teaching that corrects their misunderstanding, such as that there is only one God (not the 330 million that they used to believe they had). And they respond to understanding Him as being loving, merciful and compassionate. There is something about their past experience of fear of their former gods that inhibits a right concept and understanding of God as their heavenly Father, but their new discovery and changed lives become a wonderful testimony to share.

Unwittingly, we have stumbled on one process of leadership training that works. You have heard that in giving one a fish, you feed him for a day; but if you teach him to fish, you feed him for a lifetime. The training that these leaders receive to generate specific programs and Bible lessons from the weekly readings helps to solve the lack of printed Bible studies in their language. Now in response to their requests for printed Bible studies, we give them training in creating their own studies.

Correct answers to the seven day's worth of questions from the previous week's reading (as the process was being developed in our California house churches) are assigned three points each. But the bonus points are what trigger the daily reading habit. For each day that they read the Bible, they earn a bonus of 1 point per day (to discourage cramming the whole week's worth of reading the night before we meet). And if they read each day, the bonus for the seventh day of reading would jump to 20 additional points for a total of 26 points. Furthermore, we give the same number of points for reading the Bible within 20 minutes of arising – one point each day and 20 points for the seventh day. This creates two opportunities to pick up 26 points each.

I feel so blessed that even when the new Christians attending our house church meetings in southern California don't quite get all the answers right in the quizzes, they still score consistently in the top 5% because of the bonus points. The habit of meditating on scripture each day is daily reinforced and, in the context of our fellowship, it becomes a delightful experience. Each week's meeting sees attendees comparing notes and brushing up on what they've studied. It has been wonderful to observe and experience.

There is a reason that the bonus points were contrived to total 26 for each category. We created a "marathon" game by totaling our weekly points as a group, including individual marathon "miles" for points (since a marathon is 26 miles long). We would then look up on a map where the equivalent miles would have taken us from Los Angeles on the first leg, and identify a church in that area. I would contact the church pastor and we'd pray as a group for that church's needs. It's a wonderful experience that creates new friends across denominational lines.

The next week's "marathon" would proceed from that first point and keep making its way around North America. Our first joint effort took us to south of the border to Tijuana, Mexico, where we identified a Pentecostal church. We not only prayed for the pastor and congregation but organized a medical/dental free clinic to that church to serve their community. We hope that some of those who availed themselves of this service may have returned to attend church. The church is only 3 hours drive from where most of us live in the Los Angeles area, and it became an easy day's event.

You can see that the creative use of a Bible reading plan could pump new life into a group study program so that its members may grow spiritually.

That result of my assembling weekly questions that would create curiosity in our live and online classes to search for answers and to create a daily Bible reading habit is now in your hands. May God bless any reader of this collection at any level of experience – from examining the Bible for the first time to utilizing these nuggets in a group study.

+ Ray Puen
March 20, 2008

Preface to the Second Edition

The Olympics and the US presidential elections were still in the future when the first edition was published. But the topics will remain included in this expanded edition because the principle and validity of the answers are timeless.

Our mission training programs here and abroad aimed to encourage a devotional life as the most effective way of making lifestyle changes have positioned the One Year Bible in an important way. It has become all the more important in teaching journaling in order to more clearly discern the voice of the Lord and in forming a daily Bible reading habit. T

May the entries in this volume, developed from the daily reading passages, inspire the reader to explore the original.

December 12, 2008

Preface to the Third Edition

In response to an invitation in the first and second editions, some readers submitted questions to which answers are provided from the Bible. Because I extended this invitation also in my public lectures overseas, a great number of credits have foreign-sounding names. These names are credited below their questions. In several instances, I assembled all questions surrounding a lecture, such as the one on the Abomination of Desolation, to distribute. Many in the audiences in the different countries where our mission operates agreed to submit questions reflecting their interest in the subject being lectured on. I have grouped these together. I am further indebted to Frank Fowler for reviewing new material added here.

May 9, 2009

November 10, 2009 This Third Edition was adapted as an eBook for internet distribution.

Is _That_ in the Bible?

Who wrote the Bible?

The Bible states that it was given by inspiration of God. It originated with God, not in the minds of men. Those who wrote the different books of the Bible did not communicate their own ideas but wrote as they were moved by the Holy Spirit. And God spoke through the prophets many times and in various ways.

The Bible was written by about 40 different writers over a period of some 1,600 years between about 1500 BC and 100 AD. As it was the men who were inspired, not the words, the thoughts the writers expressed in their own words were the thoughts that came to them from God through inspiration.

Is _that_ in the Bible?

Yes – in 2 Timothy 3:16; Hebrews 1:1; 2 Peter 1:21

What is the sword of the Spirit?

The sword is the only offensive weapon on the list of the armor of God. The sword of the Spirit is identified as the word of God.

Yes, but which "word" – _logos_ or _rhema?_

Two Greek words, _logos_ and _rhema,_ are each translated "word." _Logos_ is the expression of a thought or simply the message. The Bible would be considered the _logos_ word. _Rhema_ is the spoken word. It communicates the message. A verse from the Bible (_logos_) would be transformed into _rhema_ when quoted. When one quotes scripture, he is wielding the sword of the Spirit, which is the *rhema* word of God. (The Greek for "word" in Eph. 6:17 is *rhema*, the spoken word of God.)

Jesus wielded the *rhema* word often. He said "It is written…" and then quoted part of the Old Testament (the available Bible of his day) to meet Satan's temptations head on. When we quote scripture, we transform *logos* into *rhema* power. This understanding invites the importance of memorizing scripture in order to be able to have it as available resource to use in resisting the enemy's temptations and repelling his attacks.

Is *that* in the Bible?

Yes – in Mathew. 4:4-10; Luke 4:1-13; Ephesians 6:13-17

What does it mean to hide the word of God?

Psalm 119:11 says "Your word I have hidden in my heart, that I might not sin against You." The Hebrew word translated "hide" means to memorize. It also means to guard well, to keep something dear and valuable. One guards something by fulfilling it. One hides the word of God in his heart by treasuring and memorizing scripture.

The standard Isaiah mentions that the Spirit of the Lord will raise against the enemy who comes in like a flood is memorized scripture. It is the same standard that Jesus used against Satan in the wilderness temptations – the word of God.

Is *that* in the Bible?

Yes – in Psalm 119:11, Isaiah 59:19, Matthew 4:4.

What were a jot and a tittle?

A jot was the smallest letter in the Greek and Hebrew alphabets, and the tittle was a tiny mark, smaller even than a punctuation mark, and was used to distinguish certain Hebrew letters.

To emphasize that He had come to uphold the law and the prophets, Jesus said that even if heaven and earth passed away, not even the smallest parts of the alphabets would be changed with regard to the law He came to fulfill. That even if heaven and earth pass away, His words would not.

Is _that_ in the Bible?

Yes – in Matthew 5:17-18; 24:35; Luke 16:17.

On which side of the two stone tablets were the Ten Commandments inscribed?

In order for the artist to communicate graphically how the two stone tablets must have looked, he draws two separate tablets side by side. That's the image with which we're most acquainted. This also provides the opportunity to divide the Ten Commandments for a visual representation of the way the Hebrews regarded the first four commandments to be man's duty to God and the last six to be man's duty to man. Result: in any of our illustrations today, the tablet on the left contains the first four commandments and the tablet on the right contains the last six.

But that's not how the original tablets were inscribed.

God wrote with His finger these timeless commands and unchangeable principles that were a transcript of His character, inscribing them on both sides – front and back – of each tablet.

Is *that* in the Bible?

Yes – in Exodus 31:18; 32:15

How many times did God write with His finger?

Once in each Testament.

Jesus is identified as the member of the Godhead who led the Israelites and who was the God of the Old Testament. (In the New Testament, He said that He had come to reveal the Father. The Father had not yet been revealed to that point.)

So He wrote with his finger twice – on the two stone tablets in the Old Testament and on the ground in the New Testament.

A woman caught in adultery was dragged before Jesus to trap Him into saying something that would impale Him either on Jewish law or Roman law. But instead of answering the people's question "But what do you say?" (referring to Moses' law that an adulterer should be stoned), Jesus stooped down and wrote on the ground the sins of the woman's accusers.

He then invited them to carry out Moses' law by saying "He who is without sin among you, let him throw a stone at her first," and then continued writing. The accusers were convicted by their conscience, perhaps looking over Jesus' shoulders to read their own sins, and one by one they left.

Finally only Jesus and the woman were left and He asked her, "Where are your accusers? Has no one condemned you?" and she said "No one, Lord." Jesus said "Neither do I condemn you; go and sin no more."

Note that when He wrote the Ten Commandments, He did it in stone; but when He listed people's sins, He wrote on the dust of the ground, which could be easily erased.

Is *that* in the Bible?

Yes – in Exodus 31:18; 32:15; 34:1, 4; John 8:3-11; 1 Corinthians 10:1-4

What did the shield representing faith look like?

Paul draws analogy for being equipped in spiritual warfare by using items of armor in the Roman army. The shield representing faith had an additional layer - this one of animal skin attached to the front of the shield. Before going into battle, soldiers would submerge their shields in water. The moisture soaked up by the animal skins would easily quench any fiery darts the enemy might launch against them.

A maneuver of the Roman army further insulated its soldiers from flaming arrows. The phalanx of soldiers would hold their shields so that those in front would position their shields in front of them, those on the left would hold their shields on their left, those on the right would hold their shields on their right and the soldiers in the middle would hold their shields above their heads, thus almost fully covering the phalanx of soldiers.

Is *that* in the Bible?

Yes – the reference is found in Ephesians 6:16, the historical details in some reference books.

How is this battle fought?

A clue is given at the end of the list - "praying always with all prayer and supplication in the Spirit..." Prayer is not part of the weaponry (it does not extend the list of the armor) but it is the means by which we do battle. The battle is fought in the battlefield of prayer and is waged by prayer.

Is *that* in the Bible?

Yes – in Ephesians 6:18

Why did David choose 5 smooth stones before facing off against Goliath?

It wasn't so he would have extra ammunition in case he missed the first time.

David was a skilled marksman with the sling and had much opportunity to sharpen that skill while shepherding his flocks. He very possibly was like the 700 select men from the tribe of Benjamin's army of whom it was said that they could sling a stone at a hair's breadth and not miss. David would not have needed all five stones.

The reason David chose five stones was because Goliath had four brothers. They were described as being the sons of the giant of Gath. Those stones were intended one for each of the giant brothers. Unfortunately, David never got to use the remaining four stones and the giant brothers escaped with their lives that day. They would be heard from later.

Is *that* in the Bible?

Yes – in Judges 20:16, 1 Samuel 17, 2 Samuel 21:22, and 1 Chronicles 20:8.

What was the consequence of David's not killing Goliath's giant brothers in the same battle?

They lived to fight David another day.

In fairness to the story, we must not forget that as soon as Goliath was felled by a well-aimed shot, the resulting uproar of victory on one side and panic on the other eliminated any further possible confrontation with each of the giants as the enemy fled. Nevertheless, here's what happened later.

As king, David met up again with these adversaries throughout his reign and they were a constant thorn on his side. In one memorable battle, he was almost killed but for the intervention of Abishai who came to his aid. David's men then sternly told him "You will no longer go to battle lest the lamp of Israel be quenched."

Is _that_ in the Bible?

Yes – in 2 Samuel 21:15-22 and 1 Chronicles 20:4-8

The application is sobering. What wasn't overcome in David's youth came back to haunt him in his adulthood. Character faults need to be overcome in youth or be battled in adulthood. Delay of that battle makes the victory harder to earn.

What did Jabez' mother mean by naming her son Jabez because she had given birth to him in pain?

The pain wasn't from childbirth. Physical pain would have been assumed for any childbirth, yet there were no other boys named Jabez. Only one.

The cause of the pain may be deduced from the arrangement of the chapter and the book which chronicles, among other matters, the genealogy of the tribes of Israel. In a culture where children proudly bore their father's name, the glaring omission of Jabez' father's name in this chapter was significant. Proverbs states that the glory of children is their father.

The rest of the chapter mentions each name as "the father of" followed by a listing of the sons' names. It was a matter of family pride to be so listed. So important was it that a man's name be passed on that if he died childless, his widow would marry the next eligible brother-in-law and the first son from that union would be considered the offspring of the dead brother in order that his name be perpetuated and not be forgotten in Israel.

It not only was a matter of family pride to be identified with a father's name, it was also a practical necessity. Genealogy rolls could be studied going back several generations to afford young people contemplating marriage a resource for comparing blood lines to avoid incestuous unions.

Therefore the omission of Jabez' father's name could imply that he had committed such a shameful act as to not be wanted to be mentioned among the names of the rest of the tribe. Any scribe recording such information would be bound to provide as accurate information as possible for later cross referencing (see for example Ezra 2:59, 62). The scribe who wrote this 1 Chronicles 4 genealogy may either have omitted Jabez' father's name on his own or was pressured by the community to do so.

The story ends on a hopeful note.

Jabez was described as being more honorable than his brothers. That sense of honor may have come from his decision to stay put in his community to redeem his father's name. His brothers, probably unwilling to fight what they deemed to be an unwinnable battle, had probably already relocated to start life anew elsewhere.

But Jabez stayed where his family had been known, in effect saying "I'm going to stay here and live down my father's reputation, be an asset to my community, engage in business with integrity, and win my community's respect, because I don't want my name any longer to mean that it brought shame to my family. I'll live honorably to earn the right for my name to be restored and for me to become respected."

His prayer for God's blessings ended in these words "... that I may not cause pain," meaning that his name may no longer be a reproach. He didn't want his name to be associated with his father's infamy. His own name would no longer be a cause of pain or shame to him after his campaign of restoration of honor, even if took a lifetime.

Because of that decision, he was rightly considered to be "more honorable than his brothers."

Is *that* in the Bible?

Yes – in Deuteronomy 25:6; 1 Chronicles 4:9-10; Proverbs 17:6.

Why did Elisha ask for a double portion of Elijah's spirit?

It wasn't so that he could have twice the anointing.

Nor should it be inferred that we can have twice the Spirit, because "God does not give the Spirit by measure." [John 3:34]

Rather, it was so that Elisha would experience having his prophetic call validated at the start of his public ministry. To understand this better, we must define what the *double portion* means.

Is *that* in the Bible?

Yes – the narrative starts in 2 Kings 2.

What was the double portion? Why was the first born given a double portion inheritance?

The double portion was a blessing associated with the birthright, a privilege given to the first born.

A father would divide his possessions by the number of sons he had, plus one. If a man had 12 sons, he would divide the inheritance by 13 and give the extra portion to the first born. This was called the double portion. (In the case of no male heirs, the inheritance would pass on to the daughters, as arbitrated in the case of Zelophehad's daughters.)

Some Bible historians believe that the second portion was necessary in order to meet the costs of the animal sacrifices. This could be the practicality of the double portion.

But it more likely was just a deserved inheritance because of primogeniture (the fact of his being the first born).

What it came to connote was the authority of leadership associated with the first born. Thus the references to "double portion" in scripture would mean the authority of the position. This was what Elisha needed from Elijah.

Remember that as they went from Gilgal to Bethel to Jericho and across the Jordan, certain sons of the prophets were observing them. Elisha was in effect saying "Validate my having been appointed your successor by giving an affirming sign (double portion) for my sake and before these witnesses."

The transaction was defined, agreed to, its terms met, and Elisha moved into his office as the new "father of Israel."

Is *that* in the Bible?

Yes – in Genesis 48:22; Numbers 27:1-8; Deuteronomy 21:17; 2 Kings 2.

Note: The double portion and birthright usually came to the first born but not always. In Joseph's case, he received the double portion, even though he was Jacob's eleventh son. But it is interesting to note that he could have been the first born son. Remember that his mother Rachel was Jacob's first choice for a wife. Jacob's choice then of Joseph for the double portion would be completely understandable.

Why was the refugee in the city of refuge allowed to go free when the high priest died?

God directed that cities of refuge be appointed – three on each side of the Jordan River – in order to provide a safe haven for those guilty of accidental homicide. The refuge could not be used by those guilty of intentional murder, but if a person accidentally killed another, he could flee to the closest city of refuge.

(To these six cities of refuge, God commanded an additional 42 cities to be given to the Levites including the "common-land" around the cities for grazing purposes, because they weren't included in the division of the land and had no real estate inheritance. These 48 cities were appointed for the Levites to live in.)

There in one of the six cities of refuge, the refugee (called in the Old Testament the "manslayer" and related to our word *manslaughter*) would find safety for the rest of his natural life or until the high priest died. Why? How was the refugee's freedom connected to the high priest?

This is a picture of what Jesus as our High Priest accomplished by His death – releasing us to freedom from the penalty of death.

Is *that* in the Bible?

Yes – in Numbers 18:24; 35:1-34; Deuteronomy 18:1; Joshua 18:7; Hebrews 8:1-6

Why did the high priest have bells sewn into his garment?

The priestly vestments were beautifully designed. God gave Moses directions to have artisans execute the exact blueprint designed for the priest's garments. There was symbolism connected with each article relating to Christ's priestly work in carrying the sins of humanity.

On the priest's shoulders were the two stones as a reminder that Aaron represented the people of Israel (the names of the twelve tribes were engraved, six each on these two stones). Into the chest piece, also referred to as breastplate, were woven the Urim and Thummim so that they would be carried over Aaron's heart when he went into the Lord's presence. These were used to determine the Lord's will. (You can read the rest of the description of this spectacular garment in Exodus 28.)

In the hem of the priestly garments were attached bells that tinkled as the priest moved about in his duties in the Holy Place. The assurance that if Aaron wore this robe he would not die further served to underscore how important that every little detail of attire was correctly in place, including the many steps of preparation to minister in the Lord's presence.

In this connection, there was one sober reminder of the need for the priest to be himself a perfect offering. A cord was tied around one of the priest's ankles, because if by some error on his part in his preparation to serve as a perfect priest he was killed before the Lord, someone could pull the cord, whose other end would be outside the Holy Place. The body would then be pulled out from the Holy Presence of the Lord. How would anyone know that the priest would be slain? The bells in the hem that would tinkle as the priest moved around would grow silent.

Because of the priest's grave and awesome responsibility, extreme care went into the preparation for his duties and we have no record of any priest ever suffering the death penalty for falling short.

Is *that* in the Bible?

No – the explanation about the cord comes from the Mishnah, not the Bible.

Yes – the rest of the details are described in Exodus 28.

(Mishnah = the early oral interpretations of the scriptures and forming the basic part of the Talmud.

Talmud = collection of Jewish law and tradition, the basis of authority in Orthodox Judaism)

Why did God require all plunder from Jericho to be His?

This might seem difficult to harmonize in light of God's instructions in Deuteronomy 20:14 – *You may enjoy the plunder from your enemies that the Lord your God has given you.*

But there is no confusion in this apparent contradiction if we understand the *first fruits* principle. Jericho represented the first fruits of the Canaan campaign. It was the first conquest in the Promised Land upon crossing the Jordan.

The first conquest was that which was directed by God and it provided Israel with the offering to demonstrate acknowledgment of God's sovereignty in the same way that they did with the first of the barley harvests. All other conquests after Jericho would yield plunder for the victors, but only this first one would be set apart as a first fruit and a first of the first fruits offering.

Is _that_ in the Bible?

Yes – in Joshua 6.

What were "first fruits"?

Proverbs 3:9 admonishes us to honor the Lord with the first fruits of our increase. God commanded His people to bring a portion of the oil from the first olives crushed, the new wine pressed from the first fruits of the vineyard, and some of the first grain. Barley was the first grain to come to harvest and a portion of that first harvest was appropriated as an offering. The sheaves for the sheaf offering also came from the first harvest. The flour was ground from the first harvest. All these could be presented as tithes and were set aside for the priests, Levites, singers, and gatekeepers.

God wanted His people to acknowledge by consecrating the first produce of the ground that He was their Creator, Giver of all good gifts, and Sustainer. For the Israelites, it was a joyful experience to enter into – to worship God with the first fruits of their increase. God was honored and Israel was blessed.

When God blessed His people, it sometimes was expressed in the abundance of grain, new wine, and oil.

Is _that_ in the Bible?

Yes – in Leviticus 23:12; Numbers 18:12; Deuteronomy 7:13; 11:14, 12:17, 14:23, 18:4; Nehemiah 10:39; 13:5, 12, Jeremiah 31:12; Hosea 2:22, Joel 2:19

In what way were these offerings misused?

Today, Masonic temples and buildings designed in such cities as Philadelphia and Washington, DC with rich background in Freemasonry have grain, new wine and olive oil buried in their foundations. But these aren't the first examples of misappropriating what was intended as an offering to God to be used for sacrifice. Israel had done the very same thing.

They used grain, new wine and oil as offerings to Baal. Finally, God said He would summon a drought on the fields and hills, including on the grain, new wine, olive oil and whatever the ground yielded. Again Israel was receiving indirect judgment by God's judgment of the ground, with specific mention being made of grain, new wine, and olive oil. And when Israel repented, God promised this blessing – "I am about to send you grain, new wine, and olive oil."

Is *that* in the Bible?

Yes – in Deuteronomy 28:51; Hosea 2:8, 22, Haggai 1:11.

Why did God not accept Cain's offering?

In the principle of offering the first fruits, Abel gave of the best and of the first, but Cain failed to do that. The narrative says that his giving was "in the process of time."

God eventually enunciated the importance of the first fruits principle and also the first of the first fruits. Even if Cain had given among the best fruit of the ground, it wasn't among the first.

Is that in the Bible?

Yes – in Genesis 4:1-5; Exodus 23:19, 34:26; Deuteronomy 15:19; 26:2, 10; Nehemiah 10:35; Ezekiel 44:30

What were the first of the first fruits?

God had specified that the firstborn males, all that opened the womb including humans, would be His, an offering that would be st apart for a specific purpose. Most of the sacrifices and offerings were designated for the support of the priestly and Levitical ministry.

God also specified the first of all the produce of the ground to be used as an offering. This the people cheerfully gave in grateful acknowledgment that God is the Creator, Sustainer, and Giver of all good gifts and in gratitude for the land in which they dwelt.

God promised to cause a blessing to rest on a person's house for giving the best of all first fruits of any kind. Not only were the first fruits to be chosen from the best of the first product of the ground but God also specifically called for the first of the first fruits. As applied today, it would be analogous to not only setting aside a tithe of our income, but writing the check for the tithe first. It isn't just any tenth of the increase, but the first tenth of the increase that is the principle behind the first of the first fruits.

The very act of bringing those first fruits to the Lord was to be considered an act of worship.

Is _that_ in the Bible?

Yes – in Exodus 13:12,15; 23:19; 34:19,26; Numbers 8:16; Deuteronomy 15:19; 26:2,10; Nehemiah 10:35; Ezekiel 44:30.

How many first born sons could a man have?

This question isn't as silly as it might sound. After all, being first can happen only once. But the definition given is that the first born was the one who opened the woman's womb. Thus a man who had multiple wives could have as many first-born sons as he had wives or concubines. Abraham had three first born sons (from Hagar, Sarah and Keturah) and Jacob had four (from Leah, Bilhah, Zilpah, and Rachel).

God claimed all first-born as His, including those of the livestock. He would later make provision for their redemption or substitution, and the Levites took the place of all first-born males.

Is _that_ in the Bible?

Yes – in Exodus 13:12, 15; 34:19; Numbers 3:44-51; 8:16.

Why did God use unclean birds (the ravens) to feed Elijah, instead of clean ones (like doves, for example)?

Elijah delivered the word of the Lord to Ahab – there would be no dew or rain except at his word. He then hid by the book Kerith, a tributary to the Jordan. There God commanded ravens to feed him bread and meat (food), and he drank water from the brook. No Jew would have touched food contaminated by an unclean animal but the birds that God commanded to bring food to Elijah weren't clean doves but ravens. Why?

Later, when the brook dried up, God directed Elijah to go outside the boundaries of Israel to be fed by a widow in Zarephath. Elijah would now be dealing with a woman, and a foreigner at that.

God was showing Elijah what He would show Peter in a later century – that He can use any person or agency to minister salvation or to carry out His purposes (including keeping people alive!), whether forbidden or not by culture or religious tradition. In so doing, He was tearing down existing prejudices and discrimination.

Is _that_ in the Bible?

Yes – in 1 Kings 17, Acts 10.

What does it mean to shake the dust off your shoes?

Under usual circumstances, Elijah would have shaken the dust off his sandals and feet upon his return from Zarephath. Any time Jews left their country, they would take extreme care upon their return not to track any foreign dust back in. They would shake the dust carefully before stepping back on their native soil.

It was to this custom that Jesus referred when He said that if His disciples were not received or their message heard, they were to depart after shaking the dust from their feet. This would consign that household to the level of foreign soil. Indeed, by comparison, it would be more tolerable for Sodom and Gomorrah in the Day of Judgment than for that city that refused the gospel.

Is _that_ in the Bible?

Yes – in Matthew 10:14-15; Mark 6:11; Luke 9:5; 10:11-12

Why did Jesus say "I don't have a demon" but not "I'm not a Samaritan"?

The exchange between Jesus and the Jews became spirited as the Jews smarted from Jesus' words. To their claim of Abraham as their father, Jesus said that they should then do the works of Abraham. They testily retorted that they weren't born of fornication – a reference to whispers about Jesus' birth. Jesus responded that if God were their Father as they claimed, they would listen to Jesus' words because He came from the Father.

This was simply too much for the self-righteous Jews who were seething with anger at His blasphemous statements. They accused Jesus "Do we not rightly say that You are a Samaritan and have a demon?"

A double epithet!

Spurred by anger, they hurled at Jesus the height of contempt they could think of. First – accuse Jesus of being a Samaritan, second – throw in demon possession for their perception of Jesus' diabolical reasoning regarding His relationship with God.

But He did not refuse to be identified as a Samaritan. Jesus, a Jew, was willing to be identified as a Samaritan. (A future parable – The Good Samaritan – will demonstrate that.) He was willing to be scorned and despised as a half-breed.

Jesus was saying for the sake of the Samaritans and other races, of the spurned, the despised, and the outcasts of society – "I am willing be a part of you. I have come to live among you, and to identify with you, so that you may find in Me the way to eternal life."

Is *that* in the Bible?

Yes – in John 8:48-49; John 14:6

What was so terrible about being a Samaritan anyway?

In 722 BC, the Assyrian army swept down on the northern kingdom to execute God's judgment. The people of Israel were taken into captivity. The land was left in the care of the people from the Assyrian kingdom who tried to establish their gods and system of worship. The few Israelites who were left behind struggled to keep their religion uncontaminated but to little avail. Their intermarriage with the heathen settlers that were brought in to repopulate the land resulted in a half-breed people and a half-breed religion.

A reform-minded king from the southern kingdom of Judah overran Israel and succeeded in reestablishing monotheism. But the Samaritans (people from the northern kingdom – named after their capital city Samaria) incorporated the heathen customs they had been exposed to into their way of life and worship. They were still of Jewish stock but as Samaritans were characterized by their belief only in the written, and not oral, Torah. Thus they were excluded from the congregation of Israel by the rabbis.

Samaritans were looked down on as having lost the purity of Judaism. They were viewed as half-breeds. They were despised. People traveling from Jerusalem north towards Galilee would go around to avoid going through Samaria.

(On one memorable occasion, Jesus departed from Judea to go to Galilee but He did what others didn't do – He went through Samaria. His action was the exception as the usual practice was to go around Samaria on any journeys between Judah and Galilee. It says "He needed to go through Samaria." That was because Jesus had a divine appointment there.)

To the Jews, being accused of being a Samaritan was an insult of the highest contempt.

Yet Jesus, a Jew, said nothing to deny he was a Samaritan. He too would suffer rejection, be despised, spat upon and denounced, and would be known as a half-breed, with all of which terms the word *Samaritan* was associated.

Is _that_ in the Bible?

Yes – in John 4:3-4, 9; 8:48-49.

Why did God not include "have dominion" when giving Noah command to repopulate the earth after the flood?

God had commanded Adam and Eve to be fruitful and multiply to fill the earth, adding that they should subdue it and have dominion over it and its creatures. That dominion was lost when man sinned. So when God surveyed the devastation on the earth from the universal flood, He gave Noah the same command to be fruitful and multiply and fill the earth.

But He left out the command to have dominion over the earth. That privilege had been forfeited when man sinned.

Happily a plan had already been made and would be put in motion. What was lost by Adam by disobedience at the tree would be recovered by the last Adam by obedience on the tree. Lost dominion would be restored. That plan was completed at Calvary.

Is _that_ in the Bible?

Yes – in Genesis 1:26; 9:1 and 1 Corinthians 15:45-49.

How did Eve open herself to deception by the serpent?

In the first place, she wandered away from her husband. Had he been with her, he might have helped to draw her away from the tempter.

Eve was enchanted by a talking serpent and, in the ensuing dialogue, she misquoted God's instructions. The serpent craftily inquired if it was true they couldn't eat of every tree of the garden. When Eve answered, she added to what God had told Adam. (These instructions were given Adam before Eve was created but as his wife, she was made aware of God's instructions and commands.)

What God had said was that they could eat of every tree of the garden except of the tree of the knowledge of good and evil, for on the day they ate of it, they would surely die. What Eve said was "God has said 'You shall not eat it, nor shall you touch it, lest you die.'"

What Eve added was "nor shall you touch it."

The serpent took advantage of this, assuring her "You will not surely die" and demonstrated by touching the fruit. Eve had unwittingly opened the door to deception and the serpent exploited it.

Is *that* in the Bible?

Yes – in Genesis 2:16-17 and 3:2-3

How could Eve be attracted to a serpent?

It would seem today that the appearance of a serpent would have caused Eve to recoil with dread. If that had been Eve's reaction, she would have avoided the serpent. But the serpent then didn't look the way it does today. It would have been one of the most beautiful of the created beings for the enemy to use it. Added to that fact, Eve was enchanted by hearing the serpent speak.

Because of the serpent's role in being used by the Tempter to deceive Eve, God cursed it, consigning it to move on its belly and eat dust. That would imply that it neither moved on its belly nor ate dust before it was cursed. In its being curse, it assumed the image we have of it today so that its appearance today would repulse man.

Is *that* in the Bible?

Yes – in Genesis 3:14

Why did God curse the ground for Adam's sake?

God avoided placing a curse directly on Adam. Instead, He placed it on the ground, perhaps in acknowledgment that Adam was made from dust. The earth which represented a part of Adam's makeup was placed under judgment. God said "Cursed is the ground for your sake."

God would later promise blessings to man for his obedience to His commands by blessing the ground, giving rain, causing a fruitful yield and prospering man's tilling of the soil. They would eat their fill and even dwell there in safety. In the same command, God also warned that if man disobeyed, the ground would not bear its expected yield, there would be no rain as the heavens would be shut up, the fruits of man's labor would be disproportionately small, and in general the land would be cursed for man's disobedience.

There was another sense in which the cursing of the ground was done for Adam's sake. By the sweat of his brow, man would toil the earth, but this exercise would prove a blessing to man.

Even here we see the redemptive mercy of God who refuses to curse the crowning act of His creation. He directs blessing and cursing instead to the ground and man indirectly receives the result of blessing or cursing. Many years later, God spoke through Moses to give a list of blessings and curses that would attend obedience or disobedience to his commandments. A large portion of them was expressed through the ground's yield.

Is _that_ in the Bible?

Yes – in Genesis 2:7; 3:17-19, 23; Leviticus 25:18-19; Deuteronomy 28:1-14, 15, 18, 42.

Were Adam and Eve vegetarians?

It wasn't until after the flood that God permitted man to eat flesh food. The world had been laid waste by the flood and there wouldn't be vegetation to provide food for a long time.

That's why there were seven pairs of clean animals in Noah's ark and only one pair each of the unclean. Up to the flood, God had provided as man's original diet the produce of the ground.

Is *that* in the Bible?

Yes – in Genesis 1:29 and 9:3.

Why did Adam and Eve sew fig leaves together?

Adam and Eve were created perfect. When they sinned, their eyes were opened for they now had the knowledge of both good and evil, and they saw their nakedness. So they gathered some fig leaves and sewed them together to make a covering.

God gave them an advance look into the plan of salvation. Instead of the garments of their own making, they received tunics which God made to clothe them. The skins came from an innocent animal which had to suffer a death it did not deserve in order to clothe man whose sin created the need for a covering.

Is *that* in the Bible?

Yes – in Genesis 2:25; 3:7, 21

What was woman's desire for her husband?

After God addressed the serpent with a curse and prophesied enmity between it and the woman and between its seed and her Seed, he next addressed all women through Eve and said that woman would experience pain in childbirth and that her desire would be for her husband and that he would rule over her.

Desire for a woman's husband would appear to be natural and expected, but would seem to be out of place in a statement that lists woman's pain and difficulties. That's because it wasn't the natural physical attraction that the word translated *desire* meant. The only other time in the Pentateuch (first five books in the Old Testament, ascribed to Moses) that the translated word *desire* is used is in the story of Cain. God warned Cain that sin lay at the door and "its desire is for you, but you should rule over it."

Another translation correctly conveys the intended meaning: "You will desire to control your husband, but he will rule over you." And, "Sin is crouching at the door, eager to control you. But you must subdue it and be its master." (Note that both *desire* and *rule* are mentioned in both passages.)

So *desire* is about control. It is an innate desire in women to control their husbands and in men to suppress or dominate their wives. What we identify in our time as women's lib and male chauvinism has in reality been an ages-old matter, going all the way back to Eden.

Is *that* in the Bible?

Yes – in Genesis 3:15-16, 4:7.

What is the remedy for "desire" and "rule"?

The curse addressed to Eve was the result of sin. God simply identified it to her. But this curse did not have to always be.

Paul in his epistles to the Ephesians and Colossians provided a remedy to wives' desire to control their husbands and to husbands' desire to dominate their wives. He urged wives to submit to their husbands, and husbands to love their wives. They are the remedy to the innate tendencies in man's and woman's hearts.

But just as God made mention first of woman's desire to control her husband, and then of man's desire to rule his wife, it is interesting to note that Paul mentions wives first ("submit") and then husbands next ("love").

Some Bible students point out that the admonition for a husband to love his wife comes easier when the wife first submits to her husband. The order of admonitions – to the wife first and then to the husband – is the same in both Ephesians and Colossians.

Is _that_ in the Bible?

Yes – in Genesis 3:16; Ephesians 5:22, 25; Colossians 3:18-19.

What did Cain's name mean?

Names had meaning, they many times reflected the owner's character, they were prophetic or were given as a sign. Maher-Shalal-Hash-Baz, the longest name in the Bible, was given as a sign that Assyria's siege against Judah was going to end soon. Adam meant *man*, Abraham meant *Father of a multitude*, Sarah meant *Princess*, Isaac, Jacob, Moses, Samuel, Isaiah, Daniel and almost every other name had a meaning. Many times God directed that certain children be given names he specified as a sign, such as Hosea's wife's children.

Cain's name had more than a meaning. It had an interesting background.

After the fall of man, God spoke a prophecy of a future descendant who would bruise the head of the serpent. This figurative language contained the first proclamation of the gospel and foreshadowed the coming of Jesus into the world. In her sorrow, Eve had looked forward to a quick fulfillment of this hope.

So when she had her first-born son, she wondered if this could be the Promised One. Imagine her sorrow when instead of living the kind of life that Eve might have considered worthy of redeeming his parents, he killed his brother Abel.

What name did Eve give her first born? In anticipation of the hope she nurtured, Eve named her son Cain and said, "I have acquired a man from the Lord." Many scholars say that a more accurate translation would be "I have acquired a man, the Lord," omitting the word *from*. Or, "With the Lord's help, I have produced a man!" She clearly had pinned her hopes on her firstborn's possibly being the Lord who would bring redemption.

Is *that* in the Bible?

Yes – in Genesis 3:15, 4:1, 17:5, 15-16; Isaiah 8:1; Hosea 1:4, 6, 8-9.

What did the name Eve mean?
John D. Deeke

Just as he had named all living creatures, Adam was called on to name his mate. He gave her the name Eve, meaning *Life* or *Living*, because she was the mother of all living. But in the sequence of the narrative, Adam named Eve only after the fall and after they were driven out of Eden.

When she was presented to him after God created her from his rib, Adam joyfully exulted "This is now bone of my bones and flesh of my flesh; She shall be called Woman, because she was taken out of Man."

In Hebrew the masculine and feminine form for Adam look very much the same. And Adam's wife's identity was also wrapped up in his name. It wasn't until later that Adam gave her the name Eve.

Is _that_ in the Bible?

Yes – in Genesis 3:20.

What do the miracles and the creation of Eve have in common?

After speaking the creation of the world out of nothing, God performed all miracles from pre-existing matter. When he told Moses what to do, he asked "What do you have in your hand?" and proceeded to use Moses' rod as an instrument for miracles. When he caused oil to fill all the widow's borrowed empty vessels, God started with the widow's jar of oil and multiplied it. When he directed Elijah to the widow of Zarephath, He used her last meal and oil to feed them for the rest of the time of the famine. When Jesus fed the

5,000 and later the 4,000, He started with what was available – some fish and loaves of bread.

Only man and woman were created with His hands. When He created man, God used the dust of the ground and when He created woman, He started with one of Adam's ribs.

Is *that* in the Bible?

Yes – in Genesis 2:7, 21-23; Exodus 4:1-3; 1 Kings 17:8-16; 2 Kings 4:1-7; Mark 6:31-44; 8:1-9.

What was the bronze serpent?

The children of Israel murmured and complained again and again. This time it was about the lack of food and water and they said that they loathed "this worthless bread", referring to God's daily provision of manna.

So the Lord sent fiery serpents among the people and their sting resulted in death. But when the people repented, the Lord directed Moses to make a bronze serpent and set it on a pole so that everyone bitten by the serpents could look on the bronze serpent on the pole and live.

Jesus referred to this event when He said that if He the Son of man be lifted up, everyone who believes in Him would have eternal life.

As with Aaron's censer, the cause of the people's problem and punishment becomes the agency by which the sin is atoned.

Is *that* in the Bible?

Yes – in Numbers 16:47, 21:8-9, John 3:14-15.

What was manna?

In answer to yet another complaint from the children of Israel, God told Moses that He would rain bread from heaven. It came in the form of fine flour that appeared in the early morning after the layer of dew lifted. It was like white coriander seed and tasted like wafers made of honey.

The people wondered what it could be and asked "What is it?" which is how *Manna* is translated. Manna could be baked or boiled.

Today the term "morning manna" refers to morning meditation on God's word. As an application, the parallels include engaging in the exercise before the dew lifted (for time, as in early), seeing the glory of the Lord in the morning (as in being transformed by one's meditation on the word), doing this before the sun melted the manna (for sequence, as before the daily duties interfere), providing satisfaction against hunger (for purpose, as in spiritual nourishment), and in gathering some each day (for consistency of habit of being in the word).

And God was the Provider who gave the people their daily bread.

Is *that* in the Bible?

Yes – in Exodus 16:7, 11-15, 21, 23, 31.

Note: Coriander is known today as Chinese parsley or in the Americas, cilantro.

What was angels' food?

The Psalmist wrote about angels' food. But if the psalms are poetry, then the author might have been using poetic license to rhapsodize about the nature of manna. He described manna as the bread of heaven and extended the metaphor by calling it angels' food, and that God commanded manna to rain down for people to eat.

Is _that_ in the Bible?

Yes – in Psalm 78:24-25, 105:40.

How was the gathering of manna a test?

The Lord told Moses that He would rain bread from heaven and that the gathering of the manna would become a test, whether the people would walk in God's law or not.

The test was in obeying the instructions God gave. The people were to gather manna early in the morning, and to gather enough for the day and not store any overnight, and to gather double on Friday because there would be no manna on the Sabbath.

Those who took these instructions lightly went hungry when they thought that they could gather anytime, because the hot sun melted any manna not gathered early or they had worms appear on any manna held overnight, which stank up the place, or they went without on the Sabbath when they failed to gather double on Friday.

Is _that_ in the Bible?

Yes – in Exodus 16:4, 20-21, 27.

How long did God supply manna?

Jehovah-Jireh (the God who Provides) faithfully and miraculously provided manna for the children of Israel for as long as they were in the wilderness – 40 years! When the next generation arrived in the Promised Land, a land that was flowing with milk and honey, there was no longer any reason to rain manna from heaven. The supply of manna ceased as soon as the people had their first meal eating the food of the land.

God was still providing, this time from the produce of the ground.

Is _that_ in the Bible?

Yes – in Exodus 16:35; Joshua 5:6, 11-12.

How many were blessed by one woman's kindness?

God blesses families for the faithfulness of parents, or even one parent. It one memorable instance, God caused the whole family of Rahab to be saved from the coming disaster to Jericho.

Rahab was a prostitute who hid in her rooftop the spies sent by Israel to scout the city. When the Israelites later stormed the city after God had caused the walls of Jericho to collapse, the two spies she had hidden earlier came back at Joshua's orders to keep their word to rescue her and all who were in her household.

The kindness shown by one person saved many.

Is *that* in the Bible?

Yes – in Joshua 2:1-14; 6:25; James 2:25.

Can employers be blessed for the sake or because of their employees?

When Joseph was sold into slavery, he ended up in the household of Potiphar, captain of Pharaoh's guard. Potiphar recognized that the Lord was with Joseph and made all that he did to prosper. From the time Joseph was made overseer, the Lord blessed Potiphar's household "for Joseph's sake."

Many years earlier, Joseph's father found similar favor with Laban. Jacob sought to leave his father-in-law Laban's home but Laban asked him to reconsider, saying "I have learned by experience that the Lord has blessed me for your sake." Jacob affirmed it, saying "The Lord has blessed you since my coming." It didn't matter that Laban was conniving and had taken advantage of Jacob, or that Potiphar was not of the household of faith.

The Lord blesses employers and companies because of the integrity and uprightness of their employees.

Is *that* in the Bible?

Yes – in Genesis 30:27, 30; 39:1-5.

Did Joseph indulge in sorcery in Egypt?

Egypt was known for its dark magical arts. Priests performed incantations, services for the dead, sorceries, etc. No doubt Joseph ran into this very visible part of Egyptian life. We don't even know if his wife, the daughter of the priest of On, brought any of these practices into their home. Whether or not Joseph actively practiced sorcery, he was involved in an incident that either demonstrated his participation in sorcery or his knowledge of it to the extent that he employed this Egyptian practice in order to orchestrate a situation for his benefit.

The situation: his brothers had come to Egypt to buy grain. Joseph immediately recognized them but they didn't recognize him. Jealous of him years earlier because of his favor with their father Jacob, and because of the prophetic dreams that he had, his brothers sold him into slavery. After spending some undeserved time in prison, he was released because of dreams God had given Pharaoh which no court magician could interpret.

Years earlier, Joseph had given correct interpretation to two of Pharaoh's staff who had fallen from favor and had been cast into prison. That incident was recalled and the butler recommended Joseph to Pharaoh. So he was summoned to interpret Pharaoh's dreams. He was rewarded with responsibilities to oversee his own proposed plan to store grain against the coming famine. Joseph rose to become second in rank only to Pharaoh in all of Egypt. In that capacity, God gave Joseph wisdom to plan and execute the stockpiling of grain through the seven years of bountiful harvests against the seven years of severe famine which would follow, which was the prophecy God had revealed to Pharaoh through dreams.

Now overseeing the distribution of grain from store-houses wisely constructed during the years of plenty, Joseph recognized his brothers who had come to buy grain. Concealing his true relationship with them but eager to know something of his father Jacob and his brother Benjamin, Joseph accused them of being spies. He treated them roughly in order to obtain from their defense a clear understanding of whether or not his father was still alive and of the well-being of his brother Benjamin.

Although Jacob wouldn't allow Benjamin to go, the realities of the great famine forced him to release the son of his old age, lamenting that he would go down to the grave mourning if Benjamin wasn't returned unharmed. Joseph was delighted to recognize his brother but concealed his true feelings.

In the dramatic unfolding of this reunion, Joseph orchestrated their return to the palace barely a day after they had started on their journey home with their newly-bought supply of grain.

The ruse that Joseph used was to have his steward put his cup of divination into Benjamin's sack of grain. Catching up with them the next morning, the steward feigned anger with the manner in which the brothers had "returned kindness with evil." He explained (using the words Joseph had coached him to) "Is not this [referring to the cup] the one from which my lord drinks, and with which he indeed practices divination?"

When they had returned to Joseph's house, he asked them "Did you not know that such a man as I can certainly practice divination?"

Did Joseph practice divination? Perhaps, perhaps not. The only certain thing we can obtain from this narrative is that Joseph used that excuse with which to create the situation to bring his brothers back.

Is _that_ in the Bible?

Yes – read the whole story in Genesis 37-50 and the magnificent way in which God was in control to preserve His people. The incident about the cup of divination is found in chapter 44.

How did Moses end up in an ark?

To stem the Hebrew population explosion, Pharaoh commanded the Hebrew midwives to kill all male births. When that failed, he resorted to murder and commanded that all male children be cast into the river.

A godly couple from the tribe of Levi disobeyed the command and hid their newborn son for three months. When she no longer could hide him, the baby's mother made an ark of bulrushes (papyrus reeds) and waterproofed it with tar and pitch, and placed the baby in it. (He would later be named Moses.) Then she allowed the ark to float in the river, anchored safely among the reeds that grew in the water.

His sister Miriam kept careful watch from a safe distance.

Is _that_ in the Bible?

Yes – in Exodus 1:22; 2:1-4

How was the baby Moses discovered?
Lozala Ferrer

The part of the river where Moses' ark was safely nestled among the water reeds must have been a place where the water was placid, perhaps set apart from the main river by a sand bar. In any event, it was an ideal place for people to come for a dip in the river.

That's exactly where Pharaoh's daughter headed. While her maidens patrolled the shore, the princess went in for a dip. That's when she saw the basket floating among the reeds. Sending a maid to get it, the princess opened the basket to discover a crying baby. Immediately understanding the situation, she said "This is one of the Hebrews' children."

An alert Miriam asked the princess if she could go get a nursemaid from among the Hebrew women and the princess said "Go." What better nursemaid than the baby's real mother? That's whom Miriam went to get and the princess asked her to raise the child for her. In time she brought the young boy to the palace and the princess named him Moses "because I drew him out of the water."

Is _that_ in the Bible?

Yes – in Exodus 2:5-10

Why was Moses in Midian?

Moses grew up a favored palace child and no doubt would someday have been groomed to be a future pharaoh. But when he came of age, he refused to be called the son of pharaoh's daughter, or (in other words) to be trained as heir apparent.

Choosing to cast his lot with God's people, he one day came to the rescue of a Hebrew being beat up by an Egyptian. After carefully making sure no one was looking, he killed the Egyptian.

The next day, he was trying to act as peacemaker between two Hebrews who were fighting. When the one in the wrong said "Who made you a prince and a judge over us? Do you intend to kill me as you killed the Egyptian?" Moses feared and fled for his life.

He ended up in Midian, a land in northwest Arabia populated by descendants of Abraham's fourth son by Keturah, his second wife. Moses rested by a well and assisted the seven daughters of Jethro, the priest of Midian, in watering their flock. Jethro (also called Reuel in some translations) invited Moses to stay with them and eventually he married Zipporah, one of Jethro's daughters.

Is _that_ in the Bible?

Yes – in Exodus 2:11-15; 25:2; Hebrews 11:24-26

Why did the burning bush not burn?

As Moses was tending Jethro's flocks, he saw an unusual sight that drew his attention. It was a bush in the desert wilderness where he led his flock of sheep to pasture. What was unusual was that the bush appeared to be burning, yet it wasn't consumed.

He soon found out why. As he approached the unexplainable phenomenon, a voice stopped him. "Moses, do not draw near this place. Take your sandals off your feet for the place where you stand is holy ground." It was the voice of God, in whose holy presence one was to assume the worshipful attitude of that culture.

That response – then in that culture as even today in the near east – was to take off one's shoes.

Is _that_ in the Bible?

Yes – in Exodus 3:1-5; Joshua 5:15.

When did a serpent swallow several other serpents?

God gave a reluctant Moses several miracles to perform in order to be validated as God's messenger. In performing some of these signs in front of the elders of the children of Israel, he would win their confidence.

The first of these was the turning of his staff into a serpent. God directed Moses to cast his shepherd's rod on the ground. When he did, the staff became a serpent. When Moses picked it up by the tail, the serpent turned back into a rod.

At God's direction, Moses repeated this demonstration before Pharaoh through Aaron's rod, but Pharaoh seemed unimpressed. Pharaoh called for the court magicians and they duplicated Aaron's act. Now there were several serpents crawling on the floor.

But then something strange happened.

There was only one real serpent, and that was the one which God had turned into a serpent from a shepherd's rod. All the others were counterfeits. To make this point, the real serpent swallowed all the other serpents.

Miracles point to God (such as in Aaron's rod turning into a serpent), and magic (which, as mimicry, creates doubt and confusion) points away from God (that was the act by the court magicians to produce counterfeit serpents). The snake was an Egyptian god and this first of miracles would trump the first of the Egyptians' many gods. There would be many more gods to topple, but there were 10 plagues coming up soon that would establish God as the true God (throughout His instructions to Moses God kept repeating that it would be so that "they may know that I am the Lord") as well as to discredit all the Egyptian gods.

Is _that_ in the Bible?

Yes – in Exodus 4:1-9; 7:1-13; 10:2.

What were the ten plagues about?

The children of Israel multiplied greatly until they were perceived to pose a threat to Egypt. So a plan was devised to keep them in constant subjugation by binding them to slavery. God heard their cries for deliverance and called Moses from the desert of Midian to go back to Egypt and lead God's people out of captivity.

But God said He would harden Pharaoh's heart so that God could perform a succession of miracles until the Egyptians would beg the children of Israel to leave. He even gave them favor with their masters so that whatever the Hebrews asked for, the Egyptians would gladly give, anything just to get rid of them.

These successive miracles came in the form of plagues. Each succeeding plague was more severe than the last one. And each succeeding plague was a sign to the Egyptians because it targeted a specific Egyptian deity by taking away the power of that deity to operate in the area that that deity was supposed to be in charge of or to be worshiped for. The plague wiped out any pretensions of that deity to be god in that area of Egyptian life.

The tenth plague was aimed at Pharaoh himself who had appropriated to himself the power to decide for life or death. But he couldn't do anything about protecting

his first-born son from death or bringing him back to life. In fact, Pharaoh's life was spared for a special reason. You see, by virtue of his being on the throne, he was a first born. But, the rabbis explain, he did not die so that he might see the strong and stretched arm of God. Then, God said, he (and the rest of Egypt) would know that He was God. You can read about this interesting series of plagues and God's orchestration of events in Exodus 5-11.

Is *that* in the Bible?

Yes – in Exodus 1:9-14; 3:7 – 11:10
Note: The children of Israel were affected by the first three plagues, but not by the last seven.

How many miracles did Egypt's sorcerers counterfeit?

When Pharaoh's magicians and sorcerers counterfeited Aaron's serpent, it wasn't the only miracle that they counterfeited. Remember that the counterfeit serpents were swallowed up by Aaron's rod turned serpent.

The first two plagues also were easily duplicated by the court magicians – turning the river Nile's water into blood, and producing frogs. But with the third plague, their magic stopped and they fearfully admitted "This is the finger of God."

Is *that* in the Bible?

Yes – in Exodus 7:8-12, 22; 8:7, 18-19.

Why did the angel of death pass over the Hebrews' homes?

God declared that the last plague would be so terrible that the Egyptians would beg the Israelites to leave. That plague was the death of all first born sons in every family, and included even the first born of all animals.

The Hebrews were told they would be spared if they obeyed God's provision for them. They were to take the blood of the Passover lamb and put some of it on the doorposts and on the lintel, the horizontal beam that connected the doorposts at the top.

When the angel of death came at midnight, he would pass over all the homes that were so sprinkled with blood. Hence, the term Passover.

Is *that* in the Bible?

Yes – in Exodus 1:1-13

How many Israelites left Egypt?

Census of any kind included only men. When Jesus fed the four thousand, the record says those who ate were four thousand men, "besides women and children."

So when the number given for the Israelites leaving Egypt was set at 600,000, that number would not include women and children. Later, as a result of a census, the exact number was set at 603,550 men.

By factoring in an average number of women and children, it has been estimated that the number of Israelites who left Egypt, crossed the Red Sea and wandered in the wilderness was about two-and-a-half to three million people.

Is *that* in the Bible?

Yes – in Exodus 12:37, 38:26, Matthew 15:32-38

When did a pillar of cloud lead a multitude?

God led the Israelites during the day by a pillar of cloud which became a pillar of fire at night, to provide light and warmth. The pillar of cloud and pillar of fire never left the Israelites throughout their wilderness journey.

After the Israelites fled Egypt, the Egyptians came after them. God interposed between the Israelites and the Egyptians by a cloud that was at the same time darkness to the Egyptians but light to the Israelites

The Lord's presence through the pillar of cloud also signaled when the Israelites should move forward or establish camp. The cloud hovered over the tabernacle until it was time again to break camp and move forward, the signal for which was when the cloud would be taken up from the tabernacle.

Is _that_ in the Bible?

Yes – in Exodus 13:21-22; 14:19-20; 40:36-38.

How did water come from a rock?

David rhapsodized about streams coming out of a rock, a miracle that was frequently mentioned in poetry. He was referring to God's miracle of provision in the wilderness when the Israelites camped in Rephidim. Unfortunately, there was no water there for the people to drink. This turned the people's mood from surly to mutinous and they were ready to stone Moses. Demanding water from Moses, they received a warning in that they had shifted from trusting God to expecting Moses to provide. He said "Why are you testing the Lord?"

Then Moses cried out to the Lord who directed him to take the rod with which he had struck the Nile River and to use it to strike the rock in Horeb. When he did, water gushed out of the rock. It wasn't Moses' rod that caused the water to flow (nor do dry rocks contain any water waiting to be released), but it was by a merciful God who let his miraculous provision come to a complaining people. He opened the rock, and water gushed out; it ran in the dry places like a river.

Is *that* in the Bible?

Yes – in Exodus 7:17; 17:1-6; Psalm 78:15-16, 105:41.

Why did God consider animal sacrifices to be a fragrance?

Some people recoil at the thought of a God who would seem to be pacified only by the shedding of blood and who would take pleasure in the sacrifices of innocent animals.

Perhaps seeing things from a parental perspective may help us to understand. Jesus told a parable of a prodigal son who was eagerly welcomed home by an overjoyed father who said his son who was lost was found. The same thing was involved in the sinner's offering of an animal sacrifice in the Old Testament.

Until Jesus died on the cross for our sins, God made provision for sinners to place their trust in the yet-to-come sacrifice of His Son on Calvary. The animal sacrifice and shedding of blood were all symbols that pointed to the future spotless Sacrifice of the Lamb of God – Jesus – who would take away the sins of the world. The annual sacrifices were an atonement that looked forward to Jesus becoming our Atonement. The daily sacrifices also made provision for a sinner's sins to be covered. The shedding of the blood of animals pointed to the shedding of Jesus' blood for the remission of our sins.

With what joy then did the Father receive a sinner's sacrifice and the shedding of blood that told of his sorrow for sin and his desire to be reinstated in God's family by his faith in the future Sacrifice of which his offerings were a symbol.

God said He takes no pleasure in the death of the wicked, and isn't willing that anyone should perish but that all should come to repentance. But He joyfully welcomes each sinner who appropriates for himself today the sacrifice that His Son made on Calvary on behalf of all sinners. Thus the restoration of a sinner in the Old Testament through an animal sacrifice because of his faith in the future death of the Lamb of God was to God a sweet-smelling aroma. It wasn't about the death of an animal so much as it was about the sinner being restored. This wonderful event of a sinner being restored made the animal sacrifice a sweet smelling fragrance to the Lord.

Is *that* in the Bible?

Yes – in Exodus 29:18, 25, 41; Leviticus 1:9, 13; 4:31; 8:21, 28; 17:6; 23:13, 18; Numbers 28:8, 13, 24, 27; 29:2, 8, 36; Ezekiel 18:23, 32; 33:11; Matthew 26:28; Luke 15:11-32; John 1:29; 3:16; Ephesians 5:2; Hebrews 9:22; 2 Peter 3:9.

Why did people cast lots?

God directed Aaron to cast lots for the two goats to determine which one would be the Lord's and which one would be the scapegoat. Casting lots was the ordained means to determine the Lord's will in a matter. The division of the Promised Land among the tribes was determined by casting lots after the land was surveyed.

The people saved Jonathan who had obtained a signal victory against the Philistines fighting them with only his armor bearer, when his father King Saul demanded to know why a curse had come upon the army. The king had taken a vow before the Lord that Jonathan didn't know about and he unknowingly broke it by tasting honey (the oath was that anyone eating before sundown would be killed). Casting lots determined that Jonathan was the guilty party.

Nehemiah cast lots to determine who among the priests, Levites and people would bring the wood offering into the house of the Lord, and to determine which workers would be among the one out of ten people allowed to dwell in Jerusalem during the time they were rebuilding the walls.

When Jonah fled from the Lord, he boarded a ship for Tarshish. But God sent a tempest so that the ship was about to be broken up. The mariners threw their cargo overboard to lighten the load, but to no avail. So they cast lots to determine who was the cause of trouble, and the lot fell on Jonah. Knowing that he was the cause, Jonah offered to be thrown overboard. When the men threw him into the raging sea, the tempest stopped.

Zacharias, the father of John the Baptist, had been chosen by lot for his temple duties when he experienced an angel visitation to announce the birth of his child and the name that was to be given him.

The most well-known incident involving casting of lots was for Jesus' garments, to fulfill a prophecy. The last time that any lot was cast was after Jesus' ascension and when Peter addressed one hundred twenty of Jesus' followers and said that they had to find a replacement for Judas according to the prophecy in the Psalms.

He defined that replacement to be one who had been among the followers from the beginning (Jesus' baptism by John) and who had witnessed Jesus' resurrection. The people proposed two candidates: Joseph Barsabas Justus, and

Matthias. After praying for the guidance of the Lord who could read hearts, they cast lots and the lot fell on Matthias. He was the numbered with the eleven disciples.

That would be the last mention of casting lots in the Bible. Determining God's will by casting lots would no longer be necessary because the Holy Spirit was given at Pentecost (in the following chapter, 2), who, as Jesus had promised, would lead people into all truth.

Is *that* in the Bible?

Yes – in Leviticus 16:8; Joshua 18:6, 8, 10; 1 Samuel 14:1-14, 42-45; Nehemiah 10:34, 11:1, Psalm 22:18, Jonah 1:7; Matthew 27:35; Mark 15:24; Luke 1:9, 23:34; John 16:13, 19:24; Acts 1:15-26, Acts 2.

How were Aaron and his sons anointed?

God instructed Moses to set Aaron and his sons apart for the priesthood by anointing them. The anointing oil was a special recipe God gave for special use such as this conse-cration service and it was not to be duplicated by anyone or used for other purposes.

The oil wasn't just touched to the forehead as we might anoint a person today but was generously poured on Aaron's head. In other mention of anointing, it was from a flask that the oil was poured. The anointing oil was fragrant as its composition was like that of perfume. This metaphor was used by the Psalmist to describe the pleasantness of brethren dwelling together in unity. It was as fragrant as the oil poured on Aaron's head and running down his beard, where its fragrance would be easily discerned.

Is _that_ in the Bible?

Yes – in Exodus 28:41; 29:7; 30:22-25, 30, 32, 37; 1 Samuel 10:1; 2 Kings 9:1, 3; Psalm 133:1-2.

How did Aaron die?

Because Aaron and Moses had dishonored God ("you did not hallow Me in the eyes of the children of Israel" – Numbers 20:12), they weren't allowed to lead the people into the Promised Land. When it was time for Aaron to die, God directed that he, his son Eleazar and Moses ascend Mt. Hor. Moses stripped Aaron of his garments according to God's instructions and there Aaron died.

But one matter of history needs to be accommodated.

When Miriam and Aaron spoke against Moses because of the Ethiopian woman whom he had married, the wrath of the Lord was kindled and He ordered all three to appear before Him in the tabernacle of meeting. He came in the cloud and asked Miriam and Aaron why they were not afraid to speak "against My servant Moses." God's anger was aroused against both Miriam and Aaron for their disrespectful conduct.

When the cloud departed from above the tabernacle, Miriam was leprous, as white as snow. Aaron immediately turned to Moses and pleaded that this sin not be laid "on us" - including himself in his plea. He interceded with Moses on Miriam's behalf and Moses cried out to the Lord for her healing. The Lord directed that she be shut out of the camp for seven days. The forward march was halted and not resumed until after Miriam was restored to the assembly a week later.

But what about Aaron?

No mention was made of his punishment. He knew that he was part of the judgment as evidenced by his plea "Please do not lay this sin on us, in which we have done foolishly and in which we have sinned." Note the use of *us, we,* and *we.*

As high priest, Aaron had a higher level of accountability. Higher responsibility or office demands higher level of accountability. Though it was not specifically mentioned in this narrative, it is believed that Aaron came under judgment in that the sentence of death came upon him. But his life continued because of the garments he wore in his office.

In Exodus 28, instructions were given for the construction of the priestly garments. Verse 35 specified that Aaron was to wear this robe when he ministered "that he may not die." With the sentence of death possibly on him because of the incident at Hazeroth, is it not possible that his priestly garments kept him alive to keep the word of the Lord in verse 35? Even if he had to change garments as part of his tabernacle service, his term of service would imply the continuing protection of the priestly garments. The Lord may have allowed Aaron additional years of life by His earlier provisioning through the robe and then, when it came time for Aaron to die, instructed that his garments and the protection they afforded be taken off.

Moses took away Aaron's robe and placed this symbol of priestly office on Aaron's son Eleazar. On their descent from Mt. Hor, the people saw Aaron missing and the priestly garments on his son, the next priest.

Is *that* in the Bible?

Yes - in Exodus 28:35; Numbers 12:1-16.

Who is the pearl of great price?

The usual answer people give is – "Jesus."

But Jesus wasn't the pearl of great price. Nor is that implied.

To understand this point, remember that the parable is recorded by Matthew, who was addressing his gospel to the Jews.

The pearl came from the oyster, which was an unclean animal. The pearl, therefore, would have been carefully washed with hot water or mild chemicals. Since the oyster isn't eaten, its state would not be under debate as to whether or not it was unclean.

The parable identifies a merchant (God) who finds a pearl of great value and sells all He had in order to buy it. Jesus can't be that pearl because Jesus isn't for sale, and salvation is free. But this planet and its inhabitants are precious in the Heavenly Merchant's sight and God "sold" all that He had, emptying heaven of everything in His Son Jesus, as the price for the purchase of this planet in rebellion. This planet and its inhabitants are the pearl. We are bought with a price and the great price paid for us was the death of Jesus on Calvary.

Is _that_ in the Bible?

Yes – in Matthew 13:45-46; 1 Corinthians 6:20.

When did it dawn on people that Jesus might be the promised Messiah?

The people knew the prophecies and Isaiah's definition of the Messiah. So when they saw Jesus perform miracles, the people responded with awe and amazement and wondered if this could indeed be the Son of David. This was the term Isaiah had used for the coming Messiah. While the people knew the Messiah to be the Son of David, they didn't have a name for him yet. But they soon identified Jesus to fulfill that definition.

One day a demon-possessed man was brought to Jesus who was also blind and mute. Jesus healed him so that the man both saw and spoke, prompting the multitudes to say "Could this be the Son of David?"

(It's interesting to note that another blind man – Bartimaeus – correctly called out to Jesus as Son of David where the sighted Pharisees refused to acknowledge that possibility.)

Is _that_ in the Bible?

Yes – in Isaiah 9:7; Matthew 12:22-23; Mark 10:47-48.

Why did God confuse the language of the builders of the Tower of Babel?

Only Noah's family was on earth after the flood. It took a few generations to increase the population but, sadly, the people acquired the wicked ways of the pre-flood world. As they multiplied, they decided to build a monument to themselves, a city with a tower whose top would reach above the clouds. Perhaps remembering the world's destruction by water, they may have been thinking about a way of escape should there be another flood. In any event, they were disobeying God's command to populate the whole earth.

The Lord saw what they were doing and decided to scatter the people. Their dispersion would also help populate the whole earth as God had commanded. In order to accomplish this, God confused their language. Even in some countries today, a word in one dialect could mean the exact opposite in another closely-related dialect in the same country. As workmen might have asked for a hammer and been handed a saw, the resulting chaos from this confused communication forced the people to abandon the project. Therefore the name given to the place was Babel, which means *confusion*.

The people went their separate ways, bound together in smaller groups by the new languages that they shared.

It is interesting to note that even in the pursuit of a wicked project, unity will help achieve goals. God said that because the people were united, nothing that they proposed to do would be withheld from them. They would succeed in everything they sought to do because of that unity. Therefore God confused their language and that unity was broken by the lack of clear communication. *Babel* has now come to mean meaningless sounds.

Is *that* in the Bible?

Yes – in Genesis 11:1-10.

Why was Israel admonished not to put their trust in horses or chariots?

One of the most popular breeds of horses was the Egyptian Arabian. They were loved and cherished by the noblest of officials and the desert nomad. The Prophet Mohammed taught that "every man shall love his horse." Bedouin warriors on their finest Arabian steeds proved invincible as Islam's power spread throughout the civilized world.

But thousands of years earlier, Israel had no such luxury. God had commanded them not to breed horses in order to take away any desire or excuse to return to Egypt. He specifically said "You shall not return that way again."

As the nations around Israel were equipped with horses and chariots in warfare, Israel was disadvantaged by more primitive arsenal. Therefore, they had to depend on the Lord for victory. And victory they enjoyed as the Lord went ahead of them and fought many of their battles for them. This struck fear in the hearts of Israel's enemies – the Midianites, the Perizzites, the Canaanites, the Hivites, etc.

So they learned to put their trust in the Lord and not in chariots or horses.

Later on, Solomon disobeyed this law and with his riches imported 1,400 chariots and unnumbered horses from Egypt, and entered into trade by exporting them to the Hittites and the kings of Syria. This disobedience was one of the reasons for his downfall.

Is *that* in the Bible?

Yes – in Psalm 20:7, Isaiah 31:1, Deuteronomy 17:16; 1 Kings 10:26-29; Isaiah 31:1.

How did one of Israel's enemies employ a ruse in order to negotiate a peace treaty?

Israel obediently followed the Lord's instructions to clear the land of the giants and other residents so that they could occupy their promised inheritance. God said to conquer the land in stages in order to have help in maintaining the land against wild animals.

But His instructions in dealing with the enemy were to totally annihilate them. Their uncommon success in these battles struck fear on their enemies as the Israelites' reputation went ahead of them. Many of these enemies still recalled how God led the Hebrews through dry land across the Red Sea, an event that had happened decades and generations earlier.

One enterprising nation, the Gibeonites, realizing that God was fighting for His people, and not wanting to become statistics, resorted to a ruse for their survival. They decided to ask for a peace treaty.

In order to give credence to their story, this neighboring people put on worn-out and patched clothes and shoes and carried dry and moldy bread with them, explaining that their bread had been hot from the oven when they started out many weeks earlier, giving the illusion of a great distance of travel.

Their story seemed plausible and their plea reasonable, especially when they said they had heard the name of the Lord their God and all that He had done for His people in Egypt, or even that they were willing to serve Israel as servants. Unfortunately, Joshua and the elders neglected to consult the Lord.

The Gibeonites had not come from a far-off country but lived only within a day's journey. Having unwisely entered into a covenant with them, the Israelites kept their word of providing military alliance and protection but consigned the Gibeonites to serve as woodcutters and water carriers. However, they lived in peace among the Israelites.

Is _that_ in the Bible?

Yes – in Joshua 9.

What was the consequence of breaking this treaty with the Gibeonites?

The treaty the Gibeonites negotiated with the Israelites was a covenant entered into in the name of the Lord. So the Israelites allowed them to live among God's people and would not do them any harm lest they incurred God's judgment.

Unfortunately King Saul overzealously took matters into his own hands and killed many Gibeonites. This not only broke the treaty but the bloodshed defiled the land. So the Lord brought judgment upon the land with a famine. By then David was king and he inquired of the Lord why they were suffering from a famine. The Lord said "It is because of Saul and his bloodthirsty house, because he killed the Gibeonites."

David knew that land defiled by blood could be purged of any curse upon it only by the blood of him who shed it. Sometimes righting this wrong had to be done in subsequent generations from the original wrongdoer. That was the case here and David called in the Gibeonites to determine what they would require in order for Israel to correct this wrong.

The Gibeonites demanded that seven men of Saul's descendants be delivered to them to be hanged before the Lord. David delivered the seven, but spared Mephibosheth because of his covenant with Mephibosheth's father Jonathan.

After this event had cleansed the land of bloodshed, God heeded the prayer for the land and lifted the famine. Such is the curse or blessing on a land because of blood defilement or of cleansing of such defilement. (Another incident involved the wicked queen mother Athaliah who had shed blood by killing all the royal heirs of Judah. After she was killed, the land was cleansed and enjoyed peace.)

Is *that* in the Bible?

Yes – in Numbers 35:33; Joshua 9:18-21; 2 Samuel 21; and 2 Chronicles 23:21.

Did Nebuchadnezzar know that he was an animal for 7 years?

For seven years, King Nebuchadnezzar lived like an animal, eating grass like oxen, his body made wet with the dew, his hair grown out like eagles' feathers and his nails like birds' claws. All through this time, his human understanding had left him. Why did all this happen?

He had failed to recognize that it is the Most High God of heaven who gives kingdoms to whomever He will. He thought that the kingdom of Babylon was the work of his own hands. In fact, he boasted of that very thing one day as he was walking the royal palace surveying the beautiful landscape and buildings. He said, "Is not this great Babylon that I have built for a royal dwelling by my mighty power and for the honor of my majesty?"

While he was still speaking these words, a voice fell from heaven: "King Nebuchadnezzar, the kingdom has departed from you." God described how he would be driven from his palace and would live as an animal. This was fulfilled within the hour.

Seven years later, and with an overgrowth of feathers for hair and claws for nails, Nebuchadnezzar's understanding and reasoning returned to him and he was restored to his kingdom. And now he could declare it with conviction – "Now I, Nebuchadnezzar, praise and extol and honor the King of heaven, all of whose works are truth, and His ways justice. And those who walk in pride He is able to put down."

Is _that_ in the Bible?

Yes – in Daniel 4:28-37.

How could a fiery furnace burn some people and not others?

Nebuchadnezzar made an image of gold and decreed that everyone should bow down and worship the image at the sound of the orchestra. Anyone disobeying this edict would be thrown into a fiery furnace.

Everybody bowed down except for three Hebrew young men who determined to be faithful to their early home training not to worship any graven image. The Chaldeans came forward and reported this act to King Nebuchadnezzar. In a rage, the king told them that he would give them a second chance to redeem themselves, but they assured the king that their response would be the same.

Furious, the king commanded the furnace be heated seven times hotter. He ordered certain mighty men of valor from the army to bind the Hebrew men and to cast them into the fire. The flames killed the army men but spared the Hebrew young men. Astonished, the king said "Did we not cast three men bound into the midst of the fire? Look! I see four men loose, walking in the midst of the fire; and they are not hurt, and the form of the fourth is like the Son of God."

You can read the exciting conclusion to this episode during Nebuchadnezzar's reign, in Daniel 3.

Is _that_ in the Bible?

Yes – in Exodus 20:4-5; Daniel 3.

How did Philip disappear after baptizing the Ethiopian eunuch?

Among the more interesting manifestations of the Holy Spirit are those few instances when He transported a person (and even a boat) from one place to another.

Elijah may have been transported more than once. When God sent Elijah back to King Ahab to announce that He would send rain on the earth, he ran into Obadiah who had been sent by Ahab to scour the land for water. Elijah asked Obadiah to go tell the king that he was there. This frightened Obadiah because he was certain that as soon he turned to search for the king to deliver that message, Elijah would be transported away. Apparently this occurrence in Elijah's experience was already well-known. Even the sons of the prophets referenced this manifestation of transportation when they offered to Elisha to go search for his master Elijah in case he had been transported by the Spirit elsewhere.

Ezekiel experienced the same phenomenon when the Spirit lifted him up and took him away. When Jesus' disciples got into a boat to go to Capernaum, the winds whipped up the water in the darkness as they rowed. Jesus drew near them walking on water and they were afraid. But he reassured them it was he and not to be afraid. When the disciples received him on board, the boat immediately was at the destination where they were going.

It was transportation Paul experienced (though some may confuse it with translation) when he described being caught up into Paradise.

The last instance of transportation recorded in the Bible was that of Philip being caught away by the Spirit of the Lord and taken to Azotus. Philip had been giving a Bible study to the Ethiopian eunuch who was on his way home from Jerusalem, being directed to him by an angel. After explaining that Jesus was the one written about in the Isaiah passage the eunuch was reading, Philip preached Jesus to him. The eunuch then pointed out some water they were passing and asked what was preventing him from being baptized.

Philip said that he was ready for baptism if he believed with all his heart. The eunuch then declared "I believe that Jesus Christ is the Son of God." They both joyfully went down into the water and Philip baptized him. When they came up out of the water, the Spirit of the Lord spirited Philip away. Though he saw Philip no more, the eunuch went on his way rejoicing. At that very moment, Philip was in Azotus, having been transported there by the Spirit of the Lord.

Is *that* in the Bible?

Yes – in 1 Kings 18:12; 2 Kings 2:16; Ezekiel 3:12, 14; John 6:21; Acts 8:25-40; and 2 Corinthians 12:2.

Why did the prodigal son decide to return as a hired servant?

In Luke 15, Jesus tells three parables illustrating God's unceasing effort to seek the lost. One was about the younger of two sons. He had decided to ask for an early inheritance, one that would not normally be passed on until his father's death. To Jesus' audience, this was shocking because in their culture the younger son's request would be tantamount to asking his father to die.

But he got his request and left home and family to seek his fortune in the world.

As he had friends in times of plenty, he quickly lost them when his funds ran out. The lean times stretched to where he was forced to feed swine to earn something to live on.

Imagine! He must have sunk so low that he was forced to care for animals that were an abhorrent abomination to his people. He even ate the swine's swill, times had become that rough for him.

These were times for contemplating his life and lost fortune. He reflected on how even his father's servants were better clothed and fed than he was at that low point in his life. So he made a decision.

He would swallow his pride, go home and ask his father for a job. He felt confident that he would fare much better as one of the servants than as a hungry, homeless person that he was. He even had a speech rehearsed and it contained a curiously interesting preamble.

As he rehearsed what he wanted to say, these thoughts positioned themselves first in his mind: "Father, I am no longer worthy to be called your son."

We presume this to be spoken from a sense of shame or guilt. No longer worthy to be called a son.

But to a Jewish boy, it went deeper than shame and guilt because it was an established custom of the culture that, having obtained his inheritance improperly early and leaving home (doing damage to the family reputation), he had forfeited the privileges of sonship. Had he abandoned his father's religion, the custom would have allowed the family to disown him in the strongest terms possible if they chose – they could treat him as though he never existed. They could even perform a small ceremony "burying" the disowned son as "dead." No messages sent home would be acknowledged. No conversation would be returned. He would be treated as a dead person.

Thus in telling this parable, Jesus sought to describe how deep, how high, how wide the love of the Heavenly Father is for each of his children. The father daily went out to peer into the distance, hoping that his son would someday come home. Hope ebbed and flowed through the months and years until one day, he recognized his son in the distance.

No longer clothed in the fine clothes that he wore when he left home but in tattered garments that helped to shield him nightly from the cold, his hair unkempt, and reeking of pigpen smell, he trudged wearily, hopefully, towards his former home. He wondered if he would be accepted or even allowed to ask for a servant's job.

The father never even considered the fact that his son had already received his inheritance or that he might even be considered "dead." Throwing dignity aside, he gathered the loose folds of his garment tight, the better to run, for run he did towards his son in delirious joy. The son, held back by guilt and shame, wasn't running toward his father, but the father was running towards the prodigal son. Laughing, his eyes tearing, his body shaking, the father's emotions erupted in a great upswelling of love.

Note his words as he hugged his son: "He was dead and has now returned to life" – a reference to the custom – a custom to which the father never subscribed. He rejoiced instead and gathered his son into his arms.

As for the prodigal son, all he could say of his rehearsed speech was "Father, I have sinned against both heaven and you and am no longer worthy of being called your son." That was all he got out because a loving father poured such joyous affection on him that there was no way to focus on asking to be hired as a servant. He was being restored as a son. Read the story in Luke 15.

The point of this answer to the question is that the culture of the day identified the prodigal son as one who was "dead." But though others might have left him in that state, Jesus wanted his audience to understand that a loving father refused to do that. Instead, he daily lived for the moment when he could restore his lost son to full privileges as a son again.

Is _that_ in the Bible?

Yes – The narrative is found in Luke 15:11-32, the cultural explanation is from Jewish custom.

Was the prodigal son's elder brother justified in his attitude?

The return of the prodigal wasn't received joyously by everyone, certainly not by his elder brother. To the casual reader, there might be some agreement with the way the older son felt. After all, he had stood by his father when his younger brother had left home. But his attitude was not one of son but of a servant who desires eventually to receive a reward.

Remember now that the Jewish custom provided for the older brother to receive twice the inheritance that the younger son received (this was the double portion). So to give the younger son his inheritance of one third, and two thirds of the estate to his older son as his rightful share, the father had to sell the farm. While the younger son went on to squander his inheritance in dissolute lifestyle, the older son banked his share and was hoping for an additional reward by working beyond what a son could expect, since as a son he had already received all that he would ever receive. The inheritance shares had been distributed.

But he kept on working because he was looking for a reward as a servant. His younger brother came home hoping to catch on as a servant, too, knowing that he had no longer a claim to a son's inheritance, and remembering how much better off his father's servants were than he was in a far country, herding swine. But what a contrast between the two brothers! To the Jews who valued relationships, this parable pointed out the lack of the relationship between both the sons and their father. They saw their father as an employer. They saw him as someone from whom they could earn something.

The story is not so much about the two sons as it is about their father – a father of love and compassion.

Is _that_ in the Bible?

Yes – Deuteronomy 21:17, Luke 15:11-32.

How can the dead bury their dead?

The reason Jesus told someone to let the dead bury their dead was that he had appealed to a Jewish custom to attend to the funeral of his father before he felt free to follow Jesus. The duty would have been even more incumbent on that person had he been the eldest son because then it would have been his responsibility to make the funeral arrangements.

But Jesus wanted to impress on that person and any of His other followers that there was more important work to do. For one thing, the man may have been referring to waiting for his father to die in order to discharge his family obligation before he could consider ministry. This would have been unacceptable for the urgency of kingdom matters.

So who were those who would bury the dead to whom Jesus referred? One possibility would be the professionals, the equivalent of today's mortuary staff. Another would be those who had no interest in the advance of the gospel. That would render the directive somewhat like this: Let the spiritually dead bury the physical dead.

In any event, Jesus' point was that following him and fulfilling kingdom agenda were more important than any other consideration in life – even the burying of one's dead.

Is _that_ in the Bible?

Yes – in Matthew 8:21-22; Luke 9:59-60

What was the difference between disciples and apostles?

Flor D. Bayurla

We usually number Jesus' disciples at twelve. In fact, He had many followers, or disciples.

When it came time to choose those to whom He would give special attention in mentoring, coaching, and discipling and equipping for kingdom work, He spent the night praying for divine guidance.

The next morning, He called all His followers to Himself and chose twelve which the gospels identify as apostles. These were Simon Peter, Andrew, James, John, Philip, Bartholomew, Matthew, Thomas, James, Simon the Zealot, Judas the son of James and Judas Iscariot.

Jesus continued to have many disciples but had only twelve apostles. After this event, there were many references to the twelve during and after Jesus' ministry as apostles.

Is _that_ in the Bible?

Yes – in Matthew 10:1-4; Luke 6:12-16 for their selection as apostles. Examples of their being designated "apostles" after that event are found in Mark 6:30, Luke 9:10, 17:5, 22:14, 24:10; Acts 1:2, 26; 2:37, 42, 4:33, and throughout the rest of Acts.

What was the motivation for the woman's search for the missing coin?

The three parables in Luke 15 illustrating God's search for the lost also defines three different conditions of lost-ness.

The lost coin didn't know it was lost, just as many people in the world today are not aware that they are lost or that a loving God seeks them. The lost sheep knew it was lost but was helpless in doing anything about it; it was rescued by the shepherd. The lost sheep defines those who know they are lost but are unable to find their way back except to be rescued by the Good Shepherd.

The prodigal son knew he was lost but was able to do something about it. This condition describes those who are aware of their state and can do something about it by their decision and action.

In the parable of the lost silver coin, the woman swept her whole house in diligent search of it. It must have been a very special coin to warrant throwing a party for the neighborhood at its recovery. It couldn't be for the intrinsic value of the silver, because the cost of the party would easily have exceeded that value. Perhaps the coin was part of a rare set? Then its numismatic value would increase the coin's value greatly, but not enough to justify a neighborhood block party.

So if not for its intrinsic value or its numismatic value, how about for its sentimental value? Could such a coin be that valuable to a woman?

Perhaps.

If it was part of her dowry, or if it was a wedding present from her husband, then it would have had sentimental value, and no price could be attached to that. We may not know exactly what its value was to the woman but she was more than delighted to recover it. And she invited her neighbors to rejoice with her.

Is *that* in the Bible?

Yes – in Luke 15:8-10; Ephesians 5:24, 27, 29; Revelation 19:7, 21:19.

Why could Jesus not heal certain people?

It was written that Jesus healed all who were sick, or that he laid his hands on every one of the sick and healed them, or that power went out from Him and healed them all.

But the gospel writer Mark notes a time when Jesus could do no mighty work in a certain place, except that He laid his hands on a few sick people and healed them. Only a few. Why? Jesus Himself marveled because of the people's unbelief. It was unbelief that prevented people from receiving the fullness of healing. Only a few were healed, because the general populace was unbelieving.

In fact, this situation existed immediately after Jesus explained (when people expressed surprise at Jesus' miracles, being the carpenter and son of Mary the whole neighborhood knew) that "a prophet is not without honor except in his own country, among his own relatives, and in his own house."

Jesus was in His home country when He spoke those words and it was there that He could do no mighty work because of the people's unbelief.

Is *that* in the Bible?

Yes – in Matt. 8:16, 12:15; Mark 6:1-6; Luke 4:40, 6:19.

What is the role of healing in the Great Commission?

Marco Leon

In the Mark 16 version of the Great Commission, Jesus commissioned His disciples to also cast out demons and to lay hands on the sick. When deliverance and healing are integrated in ministry, ministry becomes more effective and there is a greater response to the gospel. The word is confirmed through accompanying signs. All through the world, people respond more readily to the gospel invitation immediately after they are healed. They are most receptive then.

The multitudes with one accord heeded the things spoken by Philip, hearing and seeing the miracles which he did. In the island of Paphos, the proconsul believed, when he saw what miracles had been done. He was astonished at the teaching of the Lord but it started by his witnessing a miracle. When Peter's prayer for the healing of paralyzed Aeneas was answered, all who dwelt in that city saw him and turned to the Lord. And when Peter raised up Dorcas from the dead, it became known throughout all Joppa, and many believed on the Lord.

Today, as then, miracles will confirm the word and people will turn to the Lord.

Is _that_ in the Bible?

Yes – in Mark 16:15-18, 20; Acts 8:6, 9:34-35, 40-42, 13:12,

What was the Little Commission?
Giddell Garcia

Jesus sent His disciples out by twos, first the twelve and later the seventy, to go on a rehearsal for the Great Commission. That would be given later (after the cross) and would send them to all the world. But for now, they were limited to the lost house of Israel.

His instructions included everything that they had observed Him do – heal the sick, cast out demons, and preach the kingdom of God. That almost paralleled all that He would have them doing in the Great Commission – healing, deliverance, and preaching, plus making disciples, baptizing and instructing new believers.

The disciples returned with joy, acknowledging that even the demons were subject to them in Jesus' name. Jesus cautioned them not to rejoice in this newfound authority but rather that their names were written in heaven.

Is *that* in the Bible?

Yes – in Matthew 10:5-15; Mark 6:7-13; Luke 9:1-6; 10-1-20

Why did Jesus spit on a man?

In this instance, He was working on a miracle. Except for the act of laying hands on the sick, Jesus never used the same healing approach twice. So when a blind man was brought to him in Bethsaida, He took the man by the hand and led him out of town. Then Jesus spit on the man's eyes before laying his hands on him.

He asked the blind man if he discerned a difference. He did, but the healing apparently was incomplete because what the man saw were men like trees, walking. So Jesus laid hands on him again and made him look up. This time, the man was restored and saw everything clearly.

Is *that* in the Bible?

Yes – in Mark 8:22-26.

Why did Bartimaeus cast aside his garment?

Jesus said, "Bring him to me," referring to Bartimaeus. Bartimaeus got up from his beggar's position and cast aside his garment. Why?

Beggars would have been made to apply for a permit to beg. Their permit was a garment with a specific cut and color whose distinctive style made it readily recognizable that he was operating legally. It was with these officially-recognized beggars that the Pharisees dropped their coins to make a loud clunking noise against the beggars' metal containers. Their giving was many times preceded by a trumpet sound by the Pharisee's servant – a practice Jesus decried. He said "Don't be like them – they have their reward. But when you give, don't let the left hand know what the right hand is doing."

Bartimaeus might have heard about Jesus from reports from neighbors or family. Hope soared within him as he thrilled to the wonderful reports of Jesus' many miracles. When he shouted "Jesus, Son of David" he implied many things. The first would be that he had learned about the coming Messiah from one or both of his parents. The term Isaiah used to describe the coming Messiah was "Son of David." So Bartimaeus had a definition of the coming Messiah. He knew that, among other things, the Messiah was going to heal people, and blind Bartimaeus locked on to that hope.

But he had no name for this coming Messiah until he heard about the miracles of Jesus of Nazareth. The name Jesus was a common name in that time and so people's names were further identified by their home town. As more and more reports of miracles came to Bartimaeus, he must have determined not to let any opportunity of intersecting with the Messiah go by without his getting his healing. That's because his faith was stirred by what he had heard. Faith comes by hearing, and hearing by the word of God. He had heard the word of God in his youth, identified what the Messiah was going to do, and now he heard about Jesus' miracles and Bartimaeus put two and two together and realized that Jesus of Nazareth must be the Messiah.

He saw what the sighted leaders failed or refused to see or acknowledge. And as Jesus came towards where Bartimaeus was sitting by the roadside, Bartimaeus shouted at the top of his voice, "Jesus, Son of David, have mercy on me." In that statement containing Bartimaeus' desperate plea for healing was an acknowledgement that Jesus was the Messiah. When people attempted to hush him, Bartimaeus would not let anyone dictate to him in this his appointed time which he had many times dreamed about and looked forward to ever since he had first heard about Jesus. He shouted all the louder, "Son of David, have mercy on me." Bartimaeus' desperate faith was not to be denied.

When Jesus stopped, all the people stopped with him and a hush fell. Jesus called for him to come forward. Joyfully filled with great faith and confidence in his coming healing, he cast his garment aside. It was as though he was saying "I won't need this anymore because I'm going to be healed. Jesus is here."

His act of casting aside his garment happened before he was healed, not after. Jesus healed him after doing one more thing. He asked "What do you want me to do for you?" giving Bartimaeus the opportunity to express his faith. He replied "Rabbi, that I might receive my sight." Jesus didn't even have to lay hands on him. He said "Go your way, your faith has made you whole."

Is _that_ in the Bible?

Yes – in Matthew 6:2-4, Romans 10:17 and Mark 10:46-52

Speaking of Bartimaeus, what does his name mean?

"Bar" is the Hebrew word meaning "son of." Thus Simon Bar-Jona would be Simon the son of Jona. And Bartimaeus would be the "son of Timaeus."

In the Mark account of the healing of blind Bartimaeus, not only was his name mentioned but his father's name also was mentioned – *Bartimaeus (the son of Timaeus)*. That makes it a double mention.

Is _that_ in the Bible?

Yes – in Mark 10:46, Matthew 16:17.

How about the name Barabbas?

Well, now that you know the construction, can you extract the meaning of this Hebrew name?

Barabbas was a robber and described in the gospels as a notorious prisoner. He most likely was guilty of crimes against the Roman government.

Pilate had Jesus in front of him and was perplexed about what to do with him. Convicted of Jesus' innocence, Pilate suddenly had an idea. There was a custom – considered Roman in the gospel of Matthew and Jewish in the gospel of John – whereby a prisoner was released as part of the festivities of the occasion (it was Passover). Pilate seized upon this custom, convinced that the people would choose Jesus, in whom Pilate could find no fault, to be released if put side by side with such a criminal as Barabbas.

But he figured wrong.

The people chose Barabbas to go free!

Confounded by the unexpected response, Pilate asked what he should then do with Jesus if he set Barabbas free. Whipped into satanic fury, the chanting crowd demanded that Jesus be crucified.

And now can you extract the meaning of this Hebrew name Barabbas? Start with *bar* – "son of" and *abba* – which means "father." *Son of the Father!* What!?! Barabbas symbolizes you and me, for not only are we children of the Father, but Barabbas was set free when Jesus took his place!

O wondrous thought!

We have been set free because Jesus took our place! Suddenly the meaning of the name transcends the evil life that was lived by the man who bore the name. And so it is for us, for we all have sinned and can identify with the name Barabbas. Barabbas was worthy of death and unworthy of life. But he was set free by the death of an innocent Man.

Is *that* in the Bible?

Yes – in Matthew 27:15-26; Mark 15:6-15; Luke 23:13-25; John 18:39-40; Romans 3:23

In what group of names do we discover a hidden message?

The names of the first ten patriarchs and their meanings are: Adam – Man; Seth – Appointed; Enosh – Mortal; Kenan – Sorrow; Mahalalel – The Blessed God; Jared – Shall come down; Enoch – Teaching; Methuselah – His death shall bring; Lamech – The Despairing; Noah – Rest, or Comfort. N o w let's string them all together sequentially: *Man (is) appointed mortal sorrow; (but) the blessed God shall come down teaching (that) his death shall bring (the) despairing rest.*

Amazing!

This is advance announcement of the story of redemption hidden within a genealogy spanning thousands of years!

Is *that* in the Bible?

Yes – in Genesis 5.

Did Methuselah die before his father?
Garry B. Mupas

The patriarch Methuselah lived to 969 years. If he lived longer than any other man, how was it possible for him to die before his father?

His father was Enoch.

Enoch never died. He walked in close fellowship with God until one day at age 365 he disappeared because God took him. He was taken in that he did not see death. It was by faith that Enoch was taken up to heaven without dying for, before he was taken up, he was known as a person who pleased God.

That is how he outlived his son, the oldest man who ever lived.

Is *that* in the Bible?

Yes – in Genesis 5:21-24; Hebrews 11:5

When Jacob asked God for a blessing, why did God ask Jacob his name?

He was giving Jacob a second chance.

Jacob had been looking over his shoulder for a long time while running and hiding for his life. He was again running for his life but now he had a large family with him. Dividing his forces into two so that if the enemy attacked one half the other half could flee, he went off by himself to deal with his fears.

Such was the fear that Jacob had been living under for a long time, 20 years to be exact. Though Jacob's enemy was out there and advancing steadily, it was Jacob who had to settle matters with himself, and the most important matter to settle was to confess his true name.

You see the enemy who was advancing was his brother Esau, and it was Esau Jacob had defrauded 20 years earlier. Their father was blind in his old age and wanted to speak a father's blessing to Esau, the older of his twin sons and his favorite. He asked Esau to prepare his favorite meal from wild game so that he might enjoy it before actually speaking the blessing.

Isaac's wife Rebekah overheard this conversation. So she called her favorite son Jacob and instructed him to give her two kids from his flock. As her plan to have Jacob steal the father's blessing became clear to him, Jacob protested saying that he would be easily found out because he was smooth-skinned and his brother hairy. She effectively said "Just do as I say and trust me."

She dressed the meat and prepared it to taste like the savory venison Isaac enjoyed. She then clothed Jacob in Esau's clothes and covered Jacob's exposed skin at the hands and neck with the goats' skins.

Fully aware of the deception in which he was participating, Jacob nervously approached his father and said "My father." Isaac said "Here I am. Who are you, my son?"

Jacob tremblingly replied "I am Esau your firstborn; I have done just as you told me; please arise, sit and eat of my game, that your soul may bless me." He carried off the deception not without trepidation.

Isaac asked "How is it that you have found it so quickly, my son?"

One lie necessitated another to cover the first one. "Because the Lord your God brought it to me," Jacob explained. (*Oh, what tangled webs we weave when first we practice to deceive.*)

Isaac asked Jacob to come forward the better to feel his skin. The acid test! Because of his mother's clever ruse, Jacob passed the feel test. His father Isaac must have shaken his head when he said "The voice is Jacob's, but the hands are Esau's."

Isaac asked "Are you really my son Esau?" One last chance for redemption, but Jacob was too deep into this already.

"I am," he lied.

So Isaac ate, and after a wonderful mealtime (to Isaac, not to Jacob), Isaac asked to be kissed. As Jacob came near to kiss his father, Isaac smelled Esau's clothes (Rebekah had left nothing to chance). And Isaac blessed Jacob with the father's blessing.

(This wasn't the same as the birthright. That, too, had been stolen earlier.)

Isaac had hardly finished pronouncing the blessing on Jacob before Esau showed up. Jacob ducked out, very likely through another door. After preparing his father's savory meal, Esau brought it in to his father and invited him to sit up and eat before blessing him.

The awful realization of the grand deception hit Isaac and he tremblingly asked "Who are you?" already knowing the answer. Esau said "I am your firstborn, Esau."

"Then who," Isaac trembled exceedingly, "was the one who hunted game and gave it to me? I ate it all before you came and I have blessed him."

Struck by the realization of this terrible deception, Esau cried out in anguish, "Bless me also, O my father!" The father's blessing once given could not be recalled and Isaac said "Your brother came with deceit and has taken away your blessing."

Esau wailed "Is he not rightly named Jacob? For he has supplanted me these two times. He took away my birthright, and now he has taken away my blessing!"

Now twenty years later, Jacob wrestled with someone by the River Jabbok, not knowing it was God. Burdened by guilt and fear, he wrestled for his life. When the Man touched his hip and dislocated it, Jacob realized it was no ordinary mortal with whom he was locked in combat. As dawn broke, the Man said, "Let Me go for the day breaks." A lifetime of guilt, fear, and desire for redemption poured out in Jacob's determined answer, "I will not let you go unless You bless me!"

Strange words, for it was a blessing he sought when his troubles started twenty years earlier. But twenty years earlier, he had supplied the wrong answer to his father when queried about his identity.

Now he was being given a second chance.

"What is your name?"

This time, Jacob didn't miss. With a sense of relief, he admitted that he indeed had been a supplanter, a deceiver, a thief – all meanings of his given name.

"Jacob," he replied, unhesitatingly.

A lifetime of guilt was surrendered with that admission. He gave his name and, with it, its history. And God gave him a new name. Just as quickly as Jacob told the truth about his name, he received a blessing.

"No longer shall your name be Jacob but Israel, for you have struggled with God and with men and have prevailed."

There are blessings to those who overcome. One of them is a new name. A new identity. A new beginning. Jacob was given a second chance and he answered the question correctly.

Is _that_ in the Bible?

Yes – in Genesis 27 and 32, and Revelation 2:17.

What power is there in words?
Sony T. Myart

Rebekah had urged Jacob to steal the father's blessing intended for Esau, his older twin brother. Jacob remonstrated and said that his smooth skin would give him away. His blind father would depend on the sensation of touch and his brother Esau was hairy. No doubt Isaac would notice the difference.

Eager to not lose the opportunity her hesitant son was trying to sidestep, Rebekah assured him that nothing would go wrong, and to just leave things up to her. And if anything went wrong, she further assured him, she would be willing to take the consequences. "Let your curse be on me, my son; only obey my voice, and go, get them for me."

Them would refer to the two choice kids of the goats which she had him bring her so that she could make savory food from them to please Isaac's palate. As his wife, she knew what and how to prepare food for him.

The deception worked but Jacob ended up being sent away from home. It would be the last that Rebekah would see of her favorite son.

A few years later, Jacob and his two wives were fleeing his father-in-law Laban. Laban caught up with them and among many things, he demanded to know why Jacob had stolen his household idols. Jacob was incensed at the accusation and said "With whomever you find your gods, do not let him live." He didn't realize that Rachel had stolen those idols.

She sat on the idols while her father Laban searched the tent. She excused herself for not being able to stand but said that she was having her monthly period. Laban didn't find the idols but Jacob had spoken a curse that concerned her. Rachel died in childbearing.

There is a blessing also in words and the proper repetition of a declaration or affirmations of God's word can help a person expect better results. God…calls those things which do not exist as though they did. We can, too, declaring to be what is not yet.

Note how the power of the Lord was harnessed by what He said: "by the word of the Lord the heavens were made… For He spoke and it was done, He commanded, and it stood fast." On a smaller scale, our words have similar power. They can transform or destroy for there is power for life and death in the tongue.

Is *that* in the Bible?

Yes – in Genesis 27:9-14, 28:1-5; 31:22-35; Psalm 33:6, 9; Proverbs 18:21; Romans 4:17.

Will God bless people for telling a lie?

The ninth commandment forbids us to tell lies but there were two significant instances in scripture where people not only told lies but God blessed them as a result. It wasn't because they told lies, but because a higher principle was preserved.

The first one was when Pharaoh ordered two midwives to kill all Hebrew male babies but to spare the baby girls. They disobeyed the command and gave as an excuse that the Hebrew women were not like Egyptian women. Being lively, the Hebrew women (the midwives explained), tended to give birth before the midwives could get to them.

This was a lie but the reason given in scripture was – "...the midwives feared God." The principle was that there was a higher principle – the preservation of life, especially in this case, God's people. Killing the male children would have violated another of God's commandments. In choosing to honor God by disobeying Pharaoh, the midwives received divine favor. The narrative says "therefore God dealt well with the midwives...and...because the midwives feared God...He provided households for them."

The second instance was when spies were sent to Jericho. The harlot Rahab provided the spies protection, hiding them on the roof among stalks of flax being stored there. When it was reported to the king of Jericho that spies had come to search out the country and were in Rahab's home, he ordered her to give them up. But she told a lie. "Yes, they were here," she admitted, "but I didn't know where they were from. And before the gate was shut at dark, they left, where to, I don't know."

Then she threw in some counsel to show her "concern" and willing cooperation: If you hurry, you could still catch up with them.

The whole response was a lie to cover up the fact that she was hiding the spies. Her reason for doing so is explained in the following dialogue she had with the spies. You can read this intriguing installment of the story in Joshua 2. You will also learn how she was rewarded for protecting the spies.

The principle from these two examples points out the importance of accountability to God being higher than accountability to man. The disciples would someday express it thus: We ought to obey God rather than man.

Is *that* in the Bible?

Yes – in Exodus 1:15-22 and Joshua 2:1-1-6; Acts 5:29

Why did Tamar trick her father-in-law to have sex with her and why was she considered "more righteous" as a result?

God provided for the preservation of a man's name if he died without a male heir, by directing that his widow become the wife of the dead man's next marriageable brother. The first son produced from that subsequent marriage would belong to the woman's first husband and would carry the dead man's name to insure continuity of his line. This arrangement was called a levirate marriage.

A levirate marriage was a sacred obligation. Should a brother refuse to carry out this obligation, the widow would bring her case to the elders and in their presence remove the brother's sandal from his foot, spit in his face and say "So shall it be done to the man who will not build up his brother's house." And he would live with that shame in Israel for the rest of his life. Such was the sanctity with which the institution of levirate marriages was guarded.

Judah had three sons. The first son married Tamar but God punished him for his wicked life and he died without a son. Judah directed his second son to carry out the levirate duty by marrying Tamar but he, too, was killed by the Lord for his wicked actions. Judah then suggested that Tamar withdraw into her father's house to await the third son's maturation to marriageable age.

But Judah didn't intend to allow his son to marry Tamar for fear that he might suffer the same fate. In time (the third son also having grown), Judah went up to Timnah to his sheepshearers. Tamar, hearing this, took off her widow's garments and played the harlot, sitting in an open place but veiled, where Judah was sure to pass by on his way to Timnah. Judah, thinking her to be a harlot, propositioned her, not recognizing his daughter-in-law.

When she became pregnant, it was told Judah who then ordered her to be burned. But Tamar had Judah's items of pledge he had given her for payment and when she produced them and said that she had become pregnant by the owner of these items, Judah immediately recognized not only his signet, cord and staff and remembered the incident, but also recognized his failed promise in providing Tamar with his third-born son. Taking in the whole picture at once and understanding his failure, Judah admitted "She has been more righteous than I, because I did not give her to Shelah my son."

Is *that* in the Bible?

Yes – in Genesis 38; Deuteronomy 25:5-10

Note: Tamar gave birth to twins, the older one of whom was Perez, who became one in the line of Jesus' genealogy. Gen. 38:29 and Matt. 1:3

How strong was Samson?

Samson's name is associated with superhuman strength. His demonstrations of strength included tearing a lion apart, catching 300 foxes and tying them together in pairs by their tails and sticking a torch between each pair of tails (the foxes, when released, went into the standing grain of the Philistines and the burning torches burned their grain, vine-yards and olive groves), breaking free from being bound by two new ropes, and killing a thousand men with the jawbone of a donkey.

Delilah finally enticed Samson into revealing the source of his strength. Though he said it was from his being a Nazirite, saying "No razor has ever come upon my head...if I am shaven, then my strength will leave me...," his source of strength was not in the hair but the supernatural empow-erment by the Spirit of the Lord. In each instance of his demonstration of strength, the Bible narrative precedes it with the line "the Spirit of the Lord came upon him." This divine empowering came with his consecration to God as a Nazirite. His unshaven head was a symbol of that consecra-tion but Samson's lack of regard for his calling became his undoing. His supernatural strength left him with the cutting of his locks.

Is *that* in the Bible?

Yes – in Judges 14:6; 15:4, 13, 15; 16:17-20

Note: Samson was overpowered, his eyes gouged out and he was led to Gaza where he was bound with bronze fetters and became a grinder in the prison. But as his hair grew back, so did his strength. He was led from prison to a banquet hall for entertainment where there was much merry-making before the pagan god Dagon. Positioning himself between two pillars, Samson prayed to the Lord God to be strengthened once more. He pushed the pillars out, crying out "Let me die with the Philistines." Those who died with him in death outnumbered those whom Samson had killed in his lifetime.

What was a Nazirite?

He wasn't a resident of Nazareth – that would be a Nazarene. A Nazirite was one who took vows which, in separating himself to the Lord, resulted also in his abstention from wine, vinegar, grapes, raisins, and to avoid corpses or graves. There was one more requirement that we associate with Nazirites from the story of Samson, and that was to abstain from cutting the hair on one's head.

A Nazirite could be a man or a woman and would take vows that would last not less than 30 days. However, our association with the word is that the vow was a lifelong one, again from our understanding of the Samson story.

The usual vow was for a temporary period of time, but there were at least three Nazirites who were set apart in a special way and had lifelong vows: Samson, Samuel and John the Baptist. John the Baptist's father, Zacharias, was an example of a temporary Nazirite.

Is *that* in the Bible?

Yes – in Numbers 6:1-21; Judges 13:4-5; 1 Samuel 1:11; Luke 1:15.

What was the point of the Good Samaritan parable?

Stacy Gorgone

Neighborliness.

Jesus gave the parable in response to a query "Who is my neighbor?" The lawyer had earlier asked what he should do to inherit eternal life. Jesus in good Jewish tradition answered a question with another question "What is written in the law?' The lawyer recited the rabbinic summary of the law, known as the sh'ma: *You shall love the Lord your God with all your heart, with all your soul, with all your strength, and with all your mind, and your neighbor as yourself.*

In order to justify his lack of love for some kinds of people, the lawyer asked Jesus the definition of a neighbor. Because of the approach to scripture interpretation, there were well defined limits to any obligation, including that to love. The word "justify" suggests that the lawyer was convinced that there were some to whom the obligation for him to love might not apply. On the other hand, Jesus sought to emphasize that love is not a matter of discussion and theory but of practical demonstration.

It's true that as professional religionists, they could argue this question or any other with great skill. The less scripturally-skilled Samaritan and of lower class status did not theorize but acted. His attitude is what Jesus wanted to point out as illustration to answer the question of who was a neighbor: he who needs our help (or as he replied to Jesus "He who showed mercy.").

Is _that_ in the Bible?

Yes – in Luke 10:25-37

Note: It is easy to identify with the Samaritan in the story or to repudiate the actions of the priest and the Levite. Not so fast. Before condemning their apparent heartlessness, can't we assume from the narrative that they might have been under vows to avoid being near a dead body? (Numbers 19:11-13; also, read the entry on Nazirites above.) Of course the man lying on the road wasn't dead, but the priest and Levite might not have had the conviction that he was still alive. If there was any defilement, it would have excluded them from the Temple services.

This possibility arises from the description of their travels. The man had been travelling from Jerusalem to Jericho when he fell among thieves. The priest and Levite then were either travelling to or from Jerusalem. Jerusalem was where the priests and Levites would have travelled to in order to fulfill their vows. These two could have been on their way home from, or their way to, their period of duty. (This possible fact doesn't detract from Jesus' point of the parable.)

Can innocent people die because of the sins of the guilty?

God gave a signal victory in Israel's first military campaign in Canaan. Having crossed the Jordan River on dry ground under miraculous circumstances, the people were directed by God to conquer the walled city of Jericho by similarly super-natural means. For six days, they marched around Jericho silently, most likely to prevent any doubts to be expressed. The strange sight must have given an ominous feeling to the Jericho residents who watched in growing apprehension. On the seventh day, the Israelite army marched around Jericho seven times, letting out a mighty shout after the priests blew their rams' horns.

Jericho's walls came tumbling down.

The people rushed into the city and followed God's instructions to kill every living thing and to take no plunder. That is, all did except for one man by the name of Achan. He took a Babylonish garment and some silver and gold and buried them in his tent. The result of this sin against the Lord's command was that Israel lost the next battle against the much smaller community of Ai.

This unexpected reversal was stunning to the Israelites and to Joshua who with the elders went before the Lord with dust on their heads to ask why He had allowed this defeat. The Lord told him it was because of sin in the camp. He directed Joshua to present the people before the Lord and He would identify the guilty person by his tribe, clan and family. God identified the tribe of Judah and eventually the family of Achan.

Achan confessed his sin and told Joshua what he had taken and where they would find it. Joshua dispatched some men to dig up the loot. As punishment, Achan was stoned and his body burned. But the tragedy was that his family members suffered the punishment with him. They too were stoned and burned.

The lesson that the innocent can suffer with the guilty was not forgotten by the Israelites.

Towards the end of his life, Joshua called together the tribes of Reuben, Gad and the half tribe of Manasseh – all of whom had been promised by Moses that they could have their inheritance on the east side of the Jordan, so long as they would not avoid their responsibility of joining with the rest of the other tribes in conquering the land west of the Jordan until all tribes had received their inheritance. They faithfully kept this agreement and Joshua gave them a parting blessing as he gave them permission to return to their own promised possession. On their way home, they stopped near the Jordan River to build a large and imposing altar.

The rest of Israel heard about this and thinking that the altar had been built for worship purposes mobilized for war.

They sent a delegation representing each of the ten tribes to demand an explanation. They said "Have you not learned your lesson from the incident at Peor? To this day we are not fully cleansed of it, even after the plague that struck the entire community of the Lord."

The two-and-a-half tribes explained that the altar was not intended for worship but as a memorial to remind future generations of their right to worship the Lord and that the Jordan River would not be considered a natural barrier to prevent them from joining in worshiping the Lord.

The delegation was satisfied with their answer and blessed them before returning home to give report to the rest of Israel. The Israelites praised God and abandoned their plans of war.

But it is interesting to note one point in the delegation's demand for explanation. As they made a case that their brothers across the River not rebel against the Lord in their building an altar for worship, they reminded the two and a half tribes about their dismal defeat at Ai and its cause. They asked "Didn't divine anger fall on the entire community of Israel when Achan sinned by stealing the things set apart for the Lord?" They ended that appeal with these ominous words: "He was not the only one who died because of his sin."

It was an argument to explain why all of Israel had armed for war – they knew, based on past history, that they would be included in any judgment against the two-and-a-half tribes. Therefore they were eager to prevent any careless drift in the direction of apostasy.

Is *that* in the Bible?

Yes – in Joshua 7 and 22:21-34.

What is the difference between "confess" and "repent"?

May Grace Sisfurva

God called on His people many times to repent of their sins. We are given wonderful assurance if we confess our sins. Is there a difference between confession and repentance?

Confession is to say the same thing, to agree with. Repentance requires turning back and going in the opposite direction. Confession is acknowledging a reality. If we confess our sins, God is faithful and righteous to forgive our sins and to cleanse us from all unrighteousness.

It is possible to confess (acknowledge a condition) without experience a heart change. If a policeman pulled you over to let you know you were exceeding the speed limit and you admit it while silently fuming, you are confessing a reality – the truthfulness of the policeman's statement. You are admitting a wrong. But if you humbly add "and I'm sorry, I won't do it again" you are repenting.

Repenting starts by confessing, just as Ezra, Nehemiah, and Daniel did in interceding for God's people. But it is a full heart repentance that God desires from His people. He said through Ezekiel, "Repent and live." Jesus added, "I have...come to ccall sinners to repentance."

Confession is the response the Holy Spirit wants from us when He points out sin to us. The Holy Spirit expects us to agree with Him about what we've said or done, and to say the same thing as He does. Repentance confirms the sincerity of our confessions. By changing our minds and the direction of our lives, we show our complete agreement with the Spirit. Repentance stretches a moment under the Spirit's influence into a walk with Him in charge.

Confession is also used to acknowledge one's allegiance or to declare one's faith. Thus our salvation rests on our confession of Jesus as Lord and personal Savior.

Is _that_ in the Bible?

Yes – in Ezra 10:1; Nehemiah 1:6; Ezekiel 18:32; Daniel 9:4, 20; Luke 5:32; Romans 10:9; Philippians 2:11; 1 John 1:9

Why did David use a fourfold formula in bringing judgment upon himself?

David didn't realize he was bringing judgment upon himself until Nathan pointed to him and said, "You are the man."

Having spoken judgment upon himself, David lost 4 sons – Bathsheba's son, (2 Samuel 12), Amnon (2 Samuel 13) Absalom (2 Samuel 18) and Adonijah (1 Kings 3).

David wasn't being arbitrary in choosing the number four. This was already an established rule in Israel: If a man steals an ox or a sheep, and slaughters it or sells it, he shall restore five oxen for an ox and four sheep for a sheep." The parable that Nathan spun before David involved a sheep and so David said "he shall restore fourfold."

In the New Testament, Zacchaeus told Jesus that he demonstrated a changed heart by giving half of his goods to the poor and restoring unfairly-gotten gains fourfold (thus going beyond the Old Testament rule of restitution by twenty percent.

Is *that* in the Bible?

Yes – in Exodus 22:1; Leviticus 6:5; Numbers 5:7; 2 Samuel 12, 13, 18; 1 Kings 3, and Luke 19:8.

To how many generations did Jehu's dynasty last?
Noy Famisaran

God directed Elijah to anoint Jehu king of Israel. This commission was repeated through Elisha. Jehu was not of the royal line. Because of his zeal in ending Ahab's dynasty at the Lord's command, God promised Jehu that his sons would sit on the throne of Israel to the fourth generation. Jehoahaz, Jehu's son, reigned for seventeen years and was followed by Jehoash, who reigned for sixteen years. Then followed Jeroboam for forty one years, and Zechariah for six months, fulfilling the word of the Lord

This fifth of Israel's dynasties was also its longest, spanning more than a century. Note that God's intended reward to Jehu extended for four generations.

Is *that* in the Bible?

Yes – in 1 Kings 19:16; 2 Kings 9:1-13; 2 Kings 13:1, 10, 14:23, 15:8, 12.

How long does a covenant last?

David and Jonathan formed a covenant to look out for each other's interest and share what each had that the other lacked. At this time of his life, David had very little but Jonathan, the king's son, had everything. Jonathan also recognized God's favor on David and his appointment to be the king someday.

The covenant also called for the terms to be fulfilled in either party's descendants, so long as one party to the covenant was still alive. That, then, was the practical limit of a covenant.

Jonathan perished in battle with his father the king, and in time David ascended the throne. One day, he asked if there was any surviving descendant of the house of Saul to whom he might fulfill the terms of the covenant for Jonathan's sake.

Indeed there was, someone in his court pointed out, and his name was Mephibosheth. He was lame because when he was 5 years old, his nurse dropped him in her haste as she fled for their lives after receiving news of the battle of Jezreel where Saul and Jonathan had been killed.

David immediately directed that Mephibosheth be brought to him. Mephibosheth was understandably nervous because, as a descendant of Saul's, he feared that David would have revenge in mind. But David assured him that he intended only to show kindness for his father Jonathan's sake.

So we know that a covenant stays in effect so long as one party to that covenant is still alive.

There are many other covenants in scripture but one is of interest to us. It is the covenant God made with Abraham to bring him to a promised land, making him a great nation and that he would be a blessing. God would bless all who bless him or his descendants and curse all who curse him or his descendants, and in Abraham all the families of the earth would be blessed.

Our interest in this covenant is rooted in the fact that we are of Abraham's seed since we are Christ's, and therefore heirs according to the promise. Yes, but if we are of

Abraham's seed and heirs to the promise made to him, is that covenant still in operation today?

Yes! Though Abraham is dead, God is the other party to this covenant and He's alive! This covenant is still binding, and we are the beneficiaries of it!

Is _that_ in the Bible?

Yes – in 1 Samuel 20 and 2 Samuel 4:4; 2 Samuel 9, Genesis 12:1-3, Galatians 3:29.

When did Moses receive coaching in human resource and time management?

When his father-in-law visited him.

It was a time for family catching up. Jethro (who was also called Reuel) had brought with him Moses' wife Zipporah and their two sons Gershom and Eliezer. (Moses had likely sent his wife and sons back to Jethro sometime during the plagues in Egypt.) They exchanged stories, Moses doing most of the storytelling, especially how God miraculously delivered Israel from Egypt after Moses had left Jethro and Midian.

The next day, Jethro observed Moses at work judging the people. At the end of the exhausting day, Jethro chided him. He warned Moses that unless he changed his style, he was going to wear out. And so Jethro gave some godly counsel: choose able, God-fearing assistants who could not be bribed and place them in charge of companies of thousands, hundreds, fifties and tens, depending on their level of ability and competence. They would take care of lesser matters and Moses would handle the tough cases.

Thus Moses learned to delegate.

Later when Moses went up to the mountain with Aaron, Nadab, Abihu, Hur, Joshua and seventy of Israel's elders, Moses needed to go further alone with Joshua his assistant. He didn't hesitate to direct the elders, "If anyone has any questions, go to Aaron and Hur."

Moses had learned well the valuable lessons of delegation, division of labor, human resource management and time management.

Is _that_ in the Bible?

Yes – in Exodus 2:18; 18:1-27; 24:14; Numbers 10:29.

Is there anything God cannot do?
Garry B. Mupas

God asked Jeremiah rhetorically, "Is there anything too hard for Me?" When Sarah laughed at the idea that she would bear a child in her old age, the Lord asked Abraham, "Why did Sarah laugh, saying 'Shall I surely bear a child, since I am old?' Is anything too hard for the Lord?"

These questions imply God's Almighty power to do whatever He wants and that nothing is impossible to Him who spoke the universe into existence.

But there is something that God won't do and that is to contravene man's will. The character of God is such that He gives man the power to choose. And if man exercises his will and power of choice to do wrong, the Lord sorrowfully allows it, not because He can't do anything about it, but because it would not be consistent with His character of love to force man against his will.

Yes, there is something that God cannot do and that is to go against His nature. On one occasion, to impress this point, God sent a message to Balak through Balaam saying, "God is not a man that He should lie." It is impossible for God to lie. Or to violate any of the Ten Commandments, which are a transcript of His character.

Is *that* in the Bible?

Yes – in Genesis 18:14; Exodus 2:16; Numbers 23:19; Jeremiah 32:27; Hebrews 6:18

What is our role to be on earth?
Donald Esguerra

If we want to help limit the loss of those who do not employ their power of choice to choose eternal life, we can partner with the Holy Spirit in bringing the light of salvation into every dark corner of the world. This is universally referred to as the Great Commission.

Jesus gave His disciples this commission to take what they had learned to "teach others to observe whatsoever I have commanded you." In order to do that, they were to go into all the world, to make disciples of all peoples, and to baptize them in the name of the Father and of the Son and of the Holy Spirit.

Is *that* in the Bible?

Yes – in Matthew 28:18-20, Mark 16:15

What is the Holy Spirit's role in the Great Commission?

Benjamin Banaag

Jesus commissioned His disciples to go into all the world to make disciples, to baptize and to teach. But they were to enter into partnership with the Holy Spirit for the proclamation of the gospel.

Before Jesus said that His disciples would be witnesses in Jerusalem, Judea, Samaria and the uttermost parts of the world, He directed them to tarry in Jerusalem until they were endued with power from on high. What power? He said they would receive power when the Holy Spirit came upon them.

Finally, the Spirit and the bride together would say "Come!" The invitation is made jointly, for the power behind the gospel, the preaching or the Great Commission is the Holy Spirit.

Is _that_ in the Bible?

Yes – in Luke 24:49; Acts 1:8; Revelation 19:7; 21:9; 22:17.

What is the most effective way to evangelize?

Jessica Jalober

Jesus said that if He be lifted up, He would draw all people to Him, developing an analogy from Moses' lifting up of the serpent in the wilderness.

When Jesus engaged the Samaritan woman in conversation at the well, it resulted in the woman's leaving her waterpot right there and hurrying to the village to invite the very people she had been avoiding. She invited them to come see a man who had told her everything about her.

When they followed her, Jesus ministered to them so that they asked Him to stay two more days. Then the villagers told the woman that they now believed, not only because of her testimony but also because they themselves had heard Him.

Her role was to bring people to Jesus; it was then that Jesus was able to communicate the gospel.

Is *that* in the Bible?

Yes – in John 3:14, 4:1-45, 12:32.

What was Jehoshaphat's unusual battle plan?
Satis Thapa

Good king Jehoshaphat's reign was distinguished by reforms in the southern kingdom of Judah. One day the armies of Moab, Ammon, and Syria united to crush Judah. Jehoshaphat's response was to humble himself before the Lord and to proclaim a fast throughout all Judah.

He gathered the people to seek the Lord and, as he stood in the middle of the assembly praying, the Spirit of the Lord came upon Jahaziel. He delivered the encouraging word of the Lord and told the people and the king not to be afraid "for the battle is not yours, but God's." He explained that they would not need to fight but just to position themselves and to observe, for they would see the salvation of the Lord.

Encouraged by this assurance, Jehoshaphat bowed low with his face to the ground and, with all who had assembled, worshiped the Lord. The next morning, the king declared "Believe in the Lord your God, and you shall be established; believe His prophets, and you shall prosper," before announcing his strategy.

The Levites were to go out before the army and praise and sing – *Praise the Lord, for His mercy endures forever.* It must have been an antiphonal choir because Jehoshaphat appointed those who should sing before the Lord, and appointed those who should praise the beauty of holiness – two separate groups. As they had done the day before, they must have worshiped at a high decibel volume with "voices loud and high." When they started to sing and praise, the Lord caused the combined enemy armies to fight among themselves until all were killed. No one escaped.

This most complete victory of any warfare ever was conducted by the Lord and was triggered by worship.

Is *that* in the Bible?

Yes – in 2 Chronicles 19:4-11 and 20:1-30

What does it mean to sit at Jesus' feet?
Leni Puen

The expression that today means to be discipled by or to learn from a master originated from an incident in Jesus' ministry.

Lazarus and his two sisters Martha and Mary lived in Bethany, whose home Jesus frequently visited. It was written that he loved Lazarus and his sisters. Martha must have been the eldest of the three because she welcomed Jesus "into her house." She therefore may have most responsibly felt the pressure of the Oriental custom of hospitality. Although she complained that her sister Mary wasn't helping her, we know that Martha also sat at Jesus feet because the Luke narrative says that Mary "also" sat at Jesus feet and heard his word.

Jesus didn't criticize Martha's desire to be a proper hostess but pointed out that her concern about many things caused her to miss a higher value which he said was needed. That was to sit at the feet of Jesus and hear his word.

Is _that_ in the Bible?

Yes – in Luke 10:38-42; John 11:1,5; 12:1-2.

In what way is God a "jealous" God?
M. Pedro Cigras

In order to convey divine concepts of His relationship with man, God uses terms from human emotions and experience to illustrate His character and response. For example, He describes His faithfulness and steadfast love, His pining for us, His never-failing ardor for His people, Himself as a Lover, and us as being the supreme object of His love..

To demonstrate how He felt about Israel's going after other gods, God portrayed Himself as being "jealous" – an emotion man could readily understand, especially in the context of man's unfaithfulness (being described as a prostitute). Moses even said that Jealous was His name. It is used as a pejorative designation to be able to more clearly communicate at man's level of understanding.

Is _that_ in the Bible?

Yes – in Exodus 20:5, 34:14; Deuteronomy 5:9, 6:15, 32:16, 21; Joshua 24:19; Ezekiel 8:3, 36:5-6, 39:25; Hosea 9:1; Nahum 1:2.

Could anyone remarry his ex-spouse?
Grace A. Mason

By today's practice, people have found love at second try in remarrying an ex-spouse. But in Old Testament times, God decreed that if a person divorced his wife, then remarried and who was subsequently divorced or widowed, he would not be allowed to remarry his first wife.

Is *that* in the Bible?

Yes – in Deuteronomy 24:1-4

Why did Jesus give authority to his disciples over serpents and scorpions?

Upon the disciples' return after Jesus had sent them out by twos to the lost house of Israel, they joyfully reported that even the demons obeyed them when they used Jesus' name. Jesus' cautioned them about rejoicing over the evil spirits' obedience to them, but rather that their names were registered in heaven. However, He assured them that He had given them power over the enemy and that they could walk among snakes and scorpions. This was a reference to those same evil spirits.

Unless people today understand what the term *snakes and scorpions* means, they may make the mistake of handling snakes in a display of misplaced faith. *Snakes* and *scorpions* in the language of the day were a symbol of spiritual enemies and demonic power. Jesus has given His followers authority over them.

Is _that_ in the Bible?

Yes – in Luke 10:19.

Why did David drool?
Woot D. Uy

David had spent much time running and hiding from King Saul. Jealous of his popularity and aware that he was favored of God and in time would be the next king, Saul spent some of his royal time pursuing David when not engaged in military battles.

One of those times, David fled to Achish, the king of Gath. Gath was known as the hometown of Goliath whom David had killed with one well-aimed shot from his slingshot. Indeed, it was Goliath's sword that the priest Ahimelech had just given David along with some loaves when David was looking for provisions to feed his men.

But the servants of Achish were wary of David and asked Achish, "Is this not David the king of the land, of whom they sang to one another in dances, saying 'Saul has slain his thousands, and David his ten thousands'?"

Hearing this caution from the king's servants, David was very much afraid of Achish the king of Gath. So he changed his behavior and pretended madness, scratching on the doors of the gate and letting his saliva drool down his beard. His Oscar-worthy acting obtained the right response.

Achish ranted, "This man's insane! What on earth were you thinking of bringing him in here?" he demanded. "Do I need any madman that you have brought him to me?"

That response of course was what David hoped for and it allowed him to be left alone. He departed from there and escaped to the cave of Adullam, where family, friends, and malcontents came to join him until he had about 400 men in his band.

Is _that_ in the Bible?

Yes – in 1 Samuel 21:1-15; 22:1-2

What was David's decision about the division of spoils?
Khongkrit Inkamon

David found favor with Philistine King Achish a second time around as he continued to flee from King Saul's sight. David served well in Achish' court, living in Ziklag and going on forays to attack cities in Philistine territory, making sure that there were no survivors to give him away.

He acquitted himself well so that he became part of Achish' army. But the king's military advisers were not happy with the potential danger in David's turning against Achish in battle in order to obtain favor in Israel and King Saul. So Achish sent David away in peace. But while they were away from their Ziklag bivouac, the Amalekites came and burned down their whole encampment and carried away all who were there.

David and his men lifted their voices and wept until they had no more power to weep. His men were greatly distressed and spoke of stoning David because of the loss of their wives and daughters. But David encouraged himself in the Lord his God. Inquiring of the Lord, David was assured of victory and to pursue the enemy for he would overtake them and recover all.

They did just that.

But 200 of the 600 men were so weary that they could not follow David into battle, so they were allowed to stay at the Brook Besor to watch over the supplies. David's army pressed forward, overtook the enemy, won, and brought back their wives and daughters, and more than what they lost – spoils of battle.

But their spirit was wrong because they said that those who stayed behind would not participate in the spoils since they didn't go to battle with them. David stepped in and said "As his part is who goes down to the battle, so shall his part be who stays by the supplies; they shall share alike." (Today, we encourage intercessors to know that they share equally in the victories God gives through missionaries for whom they intercede. The intercessors are the ones who stay home and "watch over the supplies.")

When David arbitrated the arguments of his band of men, he was simply reiterating the command God had given Israel through Moses. But David now made it a statute and an ordinance in Israel.

Is *that* in the Bible?

Yes – in Numbers 31:27; 1 Samuel 27-31.

How did David handle unrest and possible mutiny?
Dawa Lama

When his men threatened to stone him, David must have feared for his life. What does a leader do in such circumstances?

He "strengthened" himself in the Lord. He encouraged himself, recounting God's past mercies and putting his confidence in the Lord to work things out.

At another low point in David's flight from King Saul, the king's son Jonathan, and David's best friend, came to strengthen David's hand in God. The word "strengthen" again is used to mean *encourage*. We are counseled to encourage one another.

Is *that* in the Bible?

Yes – in 1 Samuel 23:16, 30:6; Romans 15:5; 1 Thessalonians 5:11; Hebrews 3:13.

What happens when a person dies?
Gloria (Gigi) Guzman

The living know that they will die but the dead know not anything. Man became a living being when God formed him from the dust of the earth and breathed into his nostrils the breath of life. When a person dies, the dust will return to the earth as it was, and the spirit will return to God who gave it. That life is hid with Christ in God.

Is *that* in the Bible?

Yes – in Genesis 2:7; Ecclesiastes 3:20-21, 9:5, 12:7, Isaiah 64:8; Colossians 3:3

Where are the dead?
Rachel Pariyar

The Bible is very plain about where the dead are [see entry above]. When Jesus comes a second time, the trumpet will sound and the dead will be raised incorruptible. They are changed at this moment and will put on immortality. If immortality will be conferred at that moment, then they weren't immortal before Christ comes. If the dead are raised at that moment, then they had no life beforehand.

When the dead in Christ will rise first, then we who are alive and remain shall be caught up together with them in the clouds to meet the Lord in the air. That means that this will be the first reunion of the righteous dead and the living. Throughout all time before, the dead are described as being "asleep." Unconscious, unaware of their surroundings, dead.

Is *that* in the Bible?

Yes – in 1 Corinthians 15:20, 51-55; 1 Thessalonians 4:13-17; 2 Peter 3:4.

In what way was the gospel preached to the dead?
Ruth Pradhan

Writing to the Christians in various parts of Asia Minor who were suffering rejection in the world because of their obedience to Christ, the apostle Peter reminds them that they have a heavenly inheritance. He recalls that many now dead were alive when they heard the gospel preached, and thus were given an opportunity to live according to God in the spirit. "In the spirit" means in the realm of the Spirit. This opportunity also means that they were "judged according to men in the flesh", that is, that the issue of eternal judgment is determined by one's response to the gospel while alive.

The writer of Hebrews more clearly explains this fact: it is appointed for men to die once, but after this the judgment.

The passage by Peter doesn't mean that the gospel was preached to dead people, but that it was preached to those who were alive but had since died.

Is _that_ in the Bible?

Yes – in Hebrews 9:27; 1 Peter 4:6

Why are we not to seek out mediums and psychics?
Prabina Manandhar

God warned His people through Isaiah not to seek the dead on behalf of the living. He specifically identified mediums, wizards, who whisper and mutter. We are to avoid the occult and spiritualism. Give no regard to mediums and familiar spirits; do not seek after them, to be defiled by them. A person who turns to mediums and familiar spirits, He said would set His face against that person and cut him off from his people. God also directed that any man or woman who was a medium or who had familiar spirits should surely be put to death; they shall stone them. He defined these people - specifically – one who conjures spells, or a medium, or a spiritist, or one who calls up the dead.

God called all of these an abomination.

Is _that_ in the Bible?

Yes – in Leviticus 19:31; 20:6, 27; Deuteronomy 18:11; Isaiah 8:19.

Where did the first Christians worship?
Peter Boro

Early Christians worshiped in private homes. Church buildings did not come into use until the third century. Lydia's house served as one place where the believers met to worship. Paul sent greetings to the church that met in Pricilla and Aquila's home, and to the church that met in Archippus' home.

Is _that_ in the Bible?

Yes – in Acts 16:15, 40; Romans 16:3-5; Colossians 4:16, Philemon 1-2.

Was there a woman pastor in the Bible?
Stephen Shrestha

In the NU (the most prominent modern Greek New Testament) translation of Colossians 4:15, Nymphas, a masculine name, is spelled Nympha, a feminine name. If correct, this would be the first woman pastor of a local house church.

Is _that_ in the Bible?

Yes – in Colossians 4:15

What was the "title" of Jesus' sermons?

Satya Majhi

If Jesus were a modern-day preacher, His weekly church bulletins would have the same sermon title. Or the sub-titles would creatively point to a series bearing the same theme which He preached throughout His ministry. They would be sub-titled such as "The Mustard Seed" or "The Pearl of Great Price" or "The Sower" or "The Wheat and the Tares" or "The Hidden treasure" or "The Dragnet" or "The Lost Coin" or "The Lost Sheep" or "The Wedding Feast" or "The Good Samaritan" or "The Prodigal Son."

But they would all be tied into the same theme: The Kingdom of God.

Jesus' never-ending theme reflected in His preaching and teaching centered on these words: "The kingdom of God is at hand." The basics of Christian life are found in understanding the kingdom of God, which is not in eating or drinking (ritual performance) but in righteousness and peace and joy in the Holy Spirit. He sent His disciples on the Little Commission as an exercise in rehearsal for the later Great Commission. He gave them, in addition to healing the sick and casting out demons, this additional instruction: preach the Kingdom of God!

Is *that* in the Bible?

Yes – in Matthew 13, 20, 21:28-44; 22:1-14; Mark 1:15; 4, 12:1-11; Luke 9:2, 10:25-33; 14:16-24, 15; 16:1-13; 18:1-14; 19:12-27; 20:9-18; Romans 14:17.

Note: Mark and Luke use the term "kingdom of God" but Matthew, whose gospel addresses the Jews, defers to Jewish practice in avoiding mention of the Lord's Name, so he substitutes "heaven" for "God" – the kingdom of heaven.

Why did God allow innocent Job to suffer?

Gloria (Oyie) Banaag

The book of Job (the oldest book in the Bible) has been called "a dramatic poem framed in an epic story." The book teaches several lessons:

God is sovereign. Sovereignty means that God is all-powerful; He knows all and His decision is final; there is no one beyond Him to whom to appeal; He is the final Arbitrator. We cannot understand or reason out His workings by rational thought alone. Instead, we must exercise faith in His love.

We can understand ourselves in direct relationship to our understanding of God's character. When we understand that God wants only what's best for us, we can have peace about not knowing everything.

In times of tragedy, we face the temptation of blaming God. Even when we surrender and say "It's God's will" we ascribe to Him what He didn't intend, when we simply are reaping the result of our bad decisions. Job teaches us to bow in humility and wait patiently for God to reveal Himself and His purposes to us.

The struggle of faith continues for everyone and it is a personal one. Even when family and friends are against us, we can stand alone.

Is *that* in the Bible?

Yes – in all of Job, Jeremiah 10:10; Daniel 4:17; John 10:10.

Why did God say "You must never return to Egypt"?

Egypt represented not only the Israelites' past but also the counterfeit, the spurious and the dark magical arts.

When there was a famine in the land to which God had led Abraham, his son Isaac received directions from the Lord: it was that he wasn't to go down to Egypt. The annual flooding of the Nile provided fertile agricultural conditions where crops could be grown even during times of drought elsewhere. Isaac certainly would have found food there to buy.

But God told him not to go there. He had promised an inheritance to Abraham's descendants and so directed Isaac to dwell there in the promised land of inheritance. God was about to pour out the first of many blessings on that land. It was an opportunity to demonstrate that these blessings could not be the incidental result of agricultural process, for the land was stricken with famine. (When Israel would finally enter into their promised inheritance several centuries later, God would tell them "I gave you land that you had not worked on, I gave you towns you did not build, I gave you vineyards and olive groves for food, though you did not plant them.")

So God, to whom nothing is impossible, was eager to show that He was going to bless the land for Isaac's sake in spite of the famine. He prospered Isaac's sowing in the land in the face of evidence that a normal harvest was impossible.

In fact the yield was more than the normal yield under normal conditions, for God blessed Isaac in that same year of famine with a harvest of a hundredfold. He demonstrated as He would time and again that the land He was promising to Abraham's descendants was specially set aside for them, that it would be a place of blessings, and that in times of need He was to be their Source and Solution.

When God led Jacob's family to move to Egypt during another severe famine, He provided a fertile portion of the land (Goshen) for them in which to settle. That was favor, for the Egyptians were only too glad to apportion that place to them because they looked down on shepherds and shepherding. Over the centuries, the children of Israel (for that was Jacob's new name) multiplied so much that they were conscripted for hard labor under the pharaohs and Egyptians who feared that the children of Israel would someday outnumber the Egyptians and take over their land. God heard their cries because of their oppression and raised up a deliverer (Moses) to lead them out of Egypt.

When they left, it was a final leaving behind of everything about Egypt, their horrible experience there, and what Egypt represented in false worship. In time, the prophets would use Egypt as a metaphor for evil, sorcery, false worship and as contrast to Israel.

Is *that* in the Bible?

Yes – in Deuteronomy 17:16; Genesis 26:1-3, 12-13, Exodus 1-13, Joshua 24:13 and Jeremiah 32:17, 27.

Why should one not muzzle an ox which is treading grain?
Gard R. Wymalife

The apostle Paul refers to this Old Testament principle and to Jesus' admonition when He underscores the principle that the laborer is worthy of his wages. Muzzling an ox while it was threshing would prevent it from eating while working. The Old Testament admonition is for laborers to be properly compensated.

Paul admonished Timothy to honor elders, especially those who labored in the word and doctrine.

Is _that_ in the Bible?

Yes – in Deuteronomy 17:6, 25:4; Matthew 10:10; Luke 10:7; 1 Timothy 5:17-18

When was R&R recommended?

The demands of secular careers or church ministries call for a time of rest and relaxation. The benefits of slowing down include the refreshment of a person's spirit and the renewal of one's energy and strength. It is in this change of pace that we can hear the Lord more clearly and enter into a more intimate relationship with Him. He invites us to "be still and know that I am God."

The more hectic our schedule is, the more our need for occasional retreats and the renewal that solitude brings.

Jesus knew the importance of this principle so He invited His disciples to "Come aside by yourselves to a deserted place and rest awhile." The verse explains why – because there were many coming and going and they (the disciples) did not even have time to eat. Even in ministry, we can very easily be robbed of time because of the demands of the multitude.

Jesus practiced going aside by Himself often for this time of renewal and He was eager that His disciples learn its importance and form the habit of doing the same.

Is *that* in the Bible?

Yes – in Matthew 14:13; Mark 3:20; 6:21.

When did stretching one's arms have life or death consequences?

The Amalekites, a nomadic tribe, came to fight Israel, and Moses sent Joshua out to meet them with a volunteer army. He also promised to watch the battle from the top of the hill, implying that encouragement would come from a distance because he was going to bring with him the rod of God in his hand.

Though they had no pre-arranged signal for its use, the rod played an important role. As though to say "Is not the battle the Lord's?" Moses purposed to hold up the rod to remind the warriors of the many times God had worked miraculously through the use of this same rod in their past, during and after the plagues in Egypt. No doubt intending to secure psychological advantage by holding up the rod so that the warriors might see it and be encouraged, Moses held his staff high and started to notice something interesting.

Whenever he raised his hands, the Israelites prevailed. Then, tiring, he'd let his hands down for a little rest and that's when the Amalekites prevailed. So Aaron and Hur rolled a stone for Moses to sit on, and each one took hold of a hand and supported them in the raised position – a posture of victory – until the battle was won at sunset.

Is *that* in the Bible?

Yes – in Exodus 17:8-16.

Note: Moses built an altar there and named it Yahweh-Nissi, which means "The Lord is my banner."

When did a man wear a veil?

Moses was privileged above all others in the intimate relationship he had with the Lord as he was allowed to speak with God as a man might speak to another. He was in the presence of the Lord so much that on one memorable occasion when he spent days on Mt. Sinai being with God, his face shone with God's glory.

He wasn't aware that being in God's presence had created this phenomenon until he descended from that mountaintop experience and the people were afraid to come near him, much in the same way that they were terrified at Mt. Sinai when God spoke the Ten Commandments accompanied by a mighty display of power. So Moses put on a veil to shield the people from the brightness of God's reflected glory.

He took it off when going back into the Lord's presence but put it back on when he returned to the people. Paul referred to this event when he wrote that we would someday behold the glory of the Lord with unveiled face and experience a similar transformation by the Spirit of the Lord.

Is *that* in the Bible?

Yes – in Exodus 34:29-35; 2 Corinthians 3:18.

Why did Jesus sit down after reading from Isaiah?

Ever mindful of His Father's timetable for Him, Jesus went to Nazareth where He had been brought up, to announce the start of His earthly ministry. As His custom was, He went into the synagogue on the Sabbath day. It was the custom for someone to read from scripture and this time, Jesus took that role. He was handed the book of Isaiah and he turned to Isaiah 61.

Upon finishing the reading, He closed the book and gave it back to the attendant. Then He did what to us would have looked like a very strange thing to do. He sat down!

But that was precisely what He was expected to do. The sermon wasn't done, it had just begun!

The custom of the times was that the rabbi who would exposit the word would sit down and teach from that position. The biblical account also implies this. It said that all eyes in the synagogue were fixed on Jesus. That would be expected because they were now waiting for Him to say something.

He did and what He said was very important: *Today this scripture is fulfilled in your hearing*. This was the announcement of His ministry. He spoke it as part of the "sermon." And in the custom of the day, He delivered it sitting down.

(See also Luke 5:3 – Jesus got into Simon's boat and sat down to address the multitude)

Is _that_ in the Bible?

Yes – in Luke 4:16-21.

Why did Reuben offer his sons to Jacob to be killed?

Joseph had been sold into slavery by his brothers but God showed him favor and he was eventually elevated to be over of all Egypt, second only to Pharaoh in authority. After seven years of plenty during which Joseph supervised the storing of grain throughout all Egypt, there followed a severe famine of seven years as God had shown Pharaoh twice in a dream which Joseph had interpreted.

The famine's severity was felt worldwide and Jacob in Canaan instructed his sons to go to Egypt to buy some grain for their families' survival. Joseph immediately recognized his brothers and was eager to know about his father Jacob and his brother Benjamin. Not knowing how the intervening years had changed his brothers, Joseph disguised his approach, speaking to them harshly and completing the disguise by speaking through an interpreter. Accusing them of being spies, he ferreted out the fact that both his father and brother were alive.

Continuing to act out the charade and now eager to see Benjamin, Joseph "accused" his brothers of telling a lie and pretended to give them an opportunity to demonstrate their innocence. He required them to prove their truthfulness by producing their younger brother Benjamin whom they had identified within their defense against Joseph's accusations. He warned that they would not be allowed to see his face again unless they produced this evidence (and he kept Simeon as hostage to further ensure the reappearance of his brothers with Benjamin).

The brothers brought home a report of this unexpected turn of events, to Jacob's consternation. *Why did you have to disclose this, anyway?* he lamented. Years earlier when the brothers threw Joseph into a pit, it was Reuben who secretly planned to set Joseph free but failed. Then in Joseph's court in Egypt, Reuben told his brothers "Did I not speak to you, saying, 'Do not sin against the boy' and you would not listen? Therefore behold, his blood is now required of us."

Reuben again stepped up and this time told his father how urgent it was for them to take Benjamin with them to Egypt if they expected to be allowed to buy grain. He expressed it in very strange terms to us: "Kill my two sons if I do not bring him back to you; put him in my hands, and I will bring him back to you."

Isn't that a curious way to express persuasion? Of what persuasive value could that offer be to Jacob? Reuben's sons were his grandsons!

The expression was their culture's way of insuring the carrying out of any proposition or of demonstrating the sincerity of the speaker's intent. David's bond of friendship with Jonathan, the king's son, protected David occasionally from the king's plans to kill David. In one of their secret meetings, David expressed his frustration and dismay at the king's continued attempts on his life and said "Show me this loyalty as my sworn friend – for we made a solemn pact before the Lord – or kill me yourself if I have sinned against your father. But please don't betray me to him!" Here David puts the burden of Jonathan's proof of sincerity by inviting him to kill David if it could be shown that he had sinned against King Saul.

Later, Abner, who had been part of Saul's kingdom and who had led Ishbosheth's troops in a plan to preserve the monarchy through Saul's line, became incensed when Ishbosheth accused him of sleeping with one of his father's concubines, and in his fury decided to throw his support David's way. He said "May God strike me and even kill me if I don't do everything I can to help David get what the Lord has promised him!"

After the war in which Joab plunged three daggers into David's son Absalom's heart while he was hanging by his hair from a tree, David sent word to Amasa to replace Joab, swearing "May God strike me and even kill me if I do not appoint you as commander of my army in his place."

So using the words *strike me* or *kill me* in proper context expressed the deepest, most sincere intent of the speaker. It was a spoken vow. Thus Reuben spoke to assure his father that he would ensure the safe conduct and return of Benjamin because he had no desire for his own sons to be killed, another way of saying "I'll make sure that that won't happen."

Is *that* in the Bible?

Yes – in Genesis 37:22,29; Genesis 41, 42; 1 Samuel 20:8; 2 Samuel 3:6-10; 2 Samuel 19:13.

What was the widow's mite?

As the rich were putting their gifts into the treasury, Jesus saw a widow putting in two mites. The mite was the smallest coin in circulation and represented the smallest denominated value. Each mite was worth about $1/128^{th}$ of a denarius, a laborer's daily wage.

Jesus drew His disciples' attention to this act and said that by comparison, the widow had put in more than the others had, because she put in all that she had. The rich gave out of their abundance but she gave out of her poverty, and she gave everything that she had.

The term today is used to indicate the smallest contribution one can make and perhaps imply the comparatively great sacrifice it represents.

Other expressions we have today which come from the Bible include receiving someone else's mantle (for leadership, ability, or authority) as in Elijah's mantle falling on Elisha from the sky. The writing of the commandments on tables of stone gives us another expression. We say that something binding or unchangeable is "written in stone." And, borrowing from Gideon's experience, we say when seeking the Lord's guidance through signs that we "put out a fleece". Then there's the act of sitting at someone's feet to drink from the fountainhead of instruction, as Mary did in Jesus' presence.

Are _they_ in the Bible?

Yes – in Exodus 34:1; Judges 6:36-40; 2 Kings 2:13; Mark 12:41-44; Luke 10:39; 21:1-4.

Why can't old wineskins hold new wine?

The context was the query by John the Baptist's disciples about the lack of fasting by Jesus' disciples. Jesus showed His authority over religious rituals the people had developed into traditions.

Then He explained that new spiritual insights could not be expected to fit into the old traditional mold. Even when given light, the overwhelming response to it would be that "the old is better."

The difficulty is that new wine teaching would so challenge the wineskin of established understanding that the old wineskin would crack. This is not to suggest that new wine is superior to old wineskins. They just need to be kept separate – new wine in new wineskins and old wine in old wineskins. What Jesus cautioned against was putting new wine in old wineskins.

Is _that_ in the Bible?

Yes – in Matthew 9:17 and Luke 5:38-39.

What did Doubting Thomas doubt?

Days of sorrow over Jesus' death gave way quickly to times of rejoicing as Jesus showed himself to his disciples. He indeed was alive and the news spread rapidly. But when Jesus' disciples saw Jesus, Thomas was missing. Of course he believed that Jesus was alive – too many disciples gave testimony to that – but Thomas greatly desired to see for himself that Jesus was alive.

He expressed that desire in terms of doubt – saying that unless he saw the print of the nails in Jesus' hands, put his finger into the print of the nails, and put his hand into his side, he would not believe. Hence, he became known as the doubting disciple.

Fair enough.

Eight days later, Jesus appeared through locked doors and stood among his disciples. He addressed Thomas first, the one who was missing the first time. "Reach your finger here and look at my hands," Jesus invited Thomas to feel and see for himself.

Thomas' response was the same as anyone's who comes into undeniable evidence of the Lord's presence – and that was to worship. "My Lord and my God!" Thomas exclaimed.

Jesus commended Thomas' belief based on being able to see the evidence for himself, but spoke a blessing on those who, never being able to see for themselves, nevertheless still believed.

Is *that* in the Bible?

Yes – in John 20:25-29.

Will our pets be in the new earth?

An easier question to deal with might be "Will we have animals in the new earth?" But Ecclesiastes denotes the destination of the animal's spirit as the earth, just as the spirit of man returns to God. That would imply that our beloved pets on earth will not be in heaven or the new earth.

There is another reason that our pets cannot be saved. We are saved by our acceptance of Jesus' atonement – His death on our behalf. We can make that choice and decision. Pets are incapable of doing that.

Is *that* in the Bible?

Yes – in Ecclesiastes 3:21; Isaiah 11:6; 65:25. Rom. 10:9.

What were the leaves of the tree good for?
Mhel Dizon

The tree referenced was the tree of life straddling the river (its split trunk rooted on both sides of the river of life that proceeds from the throne of God). Bearing a different kind of fruit each month of the year for food, its leaves were for medicine (or the healing of nations.) To this day, leaves are the best source for medicinal drugs and pharmaceuticals.

Is _that_ in the Bible?

Yes – in Ezekiel 47:12 and Revelation 22:1-2.

In what sense will we do greater things than Jesus?

It's easy to think John 14:12 to mean that we will perform greater miracles than Jesus did. But the evidence doesn't appear to support what we think Jesus meant.

For example, we are not raising the dead, walking on water, healing lepers, multiplying fish and loaves, or turning water into wine. Those are among the miracles we would have to exceed performing if we understand *greater* to mean *degree*. But the greater things that we will do will not be measured in *quality* but in *quantity*.

Jesus' ministry was confined to a relatively small place on earth and the people who came to a belief in Christ were few when compared to those who responded to Peter's Pentecost sermon. Jesus was assuring us that the reach of the gospel in our hands would be greater than what He accomplished. The number of people who come to Christ in a typical Billy Graham public meeting would easily exceed the total number of people who followed Jesus or responded to His invitation throughout His earthly ministry. It is the preaching of the kingdom and the saving of the lost to which Jesus was referring.

Further support for this is found in the reason Jesus gave for our accomplishing greater works: "because I go to the Father." This refers to the promise that His going to the Father would result in the giving of the Holy Spirit, in whose power the gospel would be preached in all the world and to all the world.

Is *that* in the Bible?

Yes – in John 14:12; 16:5-15.

Why were the first born redeemed?
Joseph Quiambao

As part of their deliverance from Egypt and the celebration of the Feast of Unleavened Bread, the Israelites received a law of the firstborn which God gave through Moses. He said that the people were to set apart to the Lord all that open the womb of their animals, specifying the males to be the Lord's. This would be a sign and opportunity to explain to future generations of God's deliverance of His people out of Egypt, out of the house of bondage.

Then when the duties in the sanctuary services were defined, God made a substitution and specified that all the firstborn males of Israel would be redeemed, or exchanged for, by the Levites. There was almost the same number of Levites for first born males, with only 273 more of the first born than there were Levites. These 273 were exchanged for money, five shekels each, which helped finance the tabernacle.

Instead of the first born males being set apart to the Lord, it was now the Levites who were set apart in their stead, with their duties being in the tabernacle services and in the transport of the tabernacle and its furnishings.

Is *that* in the Bible?

Yes – in Exodus 13:12, 15; 34:19; Numbers 3:44-51; 8:16; 18:6.

Why did Jesus spit on His own fingers?

Mikal Thapa

It was part of a healing act.

Except for laying hands on the sick, Jesus very rarely repeated a healing process. Demonstrating yet another creative process in healing a deaf man brought to Him, Jesus put His fingers into the man's ears, spat on his fingers, and touched the man's tongue. Looking up into heaven, He sighed and said, *"Ephphatha,"* which means, "Be opened!" Instantly the man could hear perfectly, and his tongue was freed so he could speak plainly!

In another miracle, this one of a man blind from birth, Jesus spat on the ground and made clay with the saliva and anointed the eyes of the blind man with the clay. He then directed the man to do one more thing to participate in his own healing by an act of obedience and faith. He was to go to the pool of Siloam to wash the clay off. He did and came back seeing.

Is *that* in the Bible?

Yes – in Mark 7:31-35; John 9:1-7

Why did Jesus tell the leper not to talk about his healing?

Grace Giespy

Jesus healed a leper while in Galilee and then admonished him not to tell anyone. Instead, He urged him to show himself to the priest according to the process prescribed by Moses, that he might be pronounced clean.

The priests and others in authority had already shown their opposition to Jesus, and had the priests known the circumstances of the healing of the leper, their hatred of Christ might have led them to render a dishonest decision. Jesus wanted the leper pronounced clean before any word of the healing could precede him and render an impartial declaration unlikely.

But the healed leper succumbed to human nature and joyfully told of his healing. This had the effect of causing people to flock to Jesus in such numbers that He was forced for a time to interrupt his ministry. He "could no longer openly enter the city, but was outside in deserted places; and they came to Him from every direction."

Is _that_ in the Bible?

Yes – in Leviticus 13:13; 14:7; Mark 1:40-45

How and why was Peter released from prison?

Herod noted how it had pleased the Jews that he had killed James with the sword, the first of the twelve apostles to be martyred. Emboldened, he proceeded to seize Peter also. However, an important Jewish festival was going on (Unleavened Bread) and so Herod threw Peter in prison intending to continue his evil schemes after Passover.

But constant prayer was offered up on Peter's behalf by the church. The intercession was non-stop. The night before Herod intended to bring Peter out, an angel showed up. He woke Peter up, who was bound by chains between two soldiers. His chains immediately fell off his hands but the guards kept sleeping.

The angel told Peter to put on his sandals, his garment, and to follow him. He did, and they went past two more guard posts, no one stopping them. The gate opened untouched and when they were down one street, immediately the angel disappeared.

When he arrived at a home where many of the church had gathered, he found them still praying. There is no record of any intercession on James' behalf and he was killed. The church mobilized for prayer when they learned that Peter had been imprisoned. And God answered their prayers.

Is *that* in the Bible?

Yes – in Acts 12:1-19.

Why did a young man die when he fell asleep during the sermon?

His name was Eutychus and he was among the church members in Troas who were listening to Paul's farewell sermon. It was more than that as Paul was going to leave the next morning. No doubt he spoke exhortation, encouragement, practical advice and godly counsel in living the Christian life. He must have had much to say because he spoke all night until daybreak.

But there was an unscheduled intermission at about midnight.

Eutychus was sitting in a window and, overcome by drowsiness, sank into a deep sleep. He fell down, and as it was from a third-story window, he also fell dead. But Paul went down, fell on the dead body and in embracing it brought it back to life. He said "Don't worry, he's alive," and resumed his talk until daybreak.

Is _that_ in the Bible?

Yes – in Acts 20:9-10

Why did Joshua have his men put their feet on the necks of the vanquished kings?

It was an ancient custom of war to have the defeated enemy lie down before the king or general of the victorious army who would proceed to place his foot on the enemy's neck.

They were also strung together and paraded behind the victorious king or general. This was referred to as a spectacle.

During this particular battle, Joshua ordered that large stones be rolled against the mouth of a cave where it was told him the five enemy kings had hidden, so that he might first finish the battle. The Lord gave Joshua a great victory that day, a battle that was waged so long that Joshua needed more hours than the day had in order to complete defeating the enemy. So Joshua commanded the sun to stand still. After the victorious battle, he returned to take care of matters with the enemy kings.

He ordered the large stones removed and the kings brought to him.

It was Joshua's privilege to make a spectacle of the five defeated enemy kings, but he graciously shared that privilege with the captains of the men of war, inviting them to put their feet on the necks of the kings. He said "Do not be afraid, nor be dismayed; be strong and of good courage; for thus the Lord will do to all your enemies against whom you fight." Joshua then struck the five kings and killed them.

This action is referred to in God's promise to make our enemies our footstool. He gladly shares his privilege of victory with us, allowing us to make a spectacle of the defeated enemy. Parading the defeated enemy strung together behind the victors was the spectacle.

David used this metaphor in his psalms, and it is sustained in the description of Christ as having disarmed the enemy and making a public spectacle of them.

Is _that_ in the Bible?

Yes – in Joshua 10:16-27; 2 Samuel 22:41, Psalm 18:40; 110:1 1 Corinthians 15:25; Colossians 2:15.

How did the sun stand still?

A day like no other before or since was the day during which Joshua battled a coalition of enemy forces.

King Adoni-zedek of Jerusalem, troubled that the great city Gibeon had entered into treaty with Israel, sent for four other kings to join him in battle against Israel. Gibeon called on their covenant agreement with Israel and Joshua responded by mobilizing Israel's forces.

God assured Joshua of victory and caused the enemy forces to be defeated, even raining large hailstones on them. More died from the hailstones than from the sword.

But the battle was as long as it was fierce and Joshua was running short of daylight. In order to finish the battle, he needed to extend the daylight and so Joshua commanded the sun to stand still –

Sun, stand still over Gibeon,
And moon, in the valley of Aijalon.

So the sun stood still and didn't go down for the span of about 24 hours, until the people had had revenge on their enemies.

Is _that_ in the Bible?

Yes – in Joshua 10:1-14.

What sign did God give to confirm promise of additional years to Hezekiah's life?

Another span of time was added during Hezekiah's day and some scientists estimate that the combined total of Joshua's lengthened day and the minutes added when Hezekiah, king of Judah, received a promise of life extension total one complete 24-hour day.

Just as God had told Aaron and Moses to get ready to die, so he sent word to Hezekiah through Isaiah to set his house in order for he was going to die. Hezekiah wept bitterly as he prayed and God told Isaiah, not yet gone out so far as the middle court, to return to the king with another message: he would be healed and live another 15 years.

Isaiah directed that a fig poultice be applied to Hezekiah's boil and Hezekiah recovered. He asked the prophet, "How will I know that I will be healed?" Isaiah gave him the choice of having the sundial's shadow move forward or backward 10 degrees as a sign. Hezekiah said that it would be an easy thing to have the shadow accelerate forward and asked instead that the shadow be turned backwards. Such a sign would be more significant.

And God, to whom nothing is impossible, caused the sundial's shadow to move back 10 degrees. The retracement of ten degrees equated to 40 minutes, the additional length for that one day.

Is _that_ in the Bible?

Yes – in 2 Kings 20:1-11; 2 Chronicles 32:24; and Isaiah 38.

Was Hezekiah's prayer one of entitlement?

Hezekiah wasn't the only one to call on God to remember his past record. A widow of the sons of the prophets came to Elisha to ask for help because she had fallen on hard times and the creditor was coming to take her two sons to pay off her accumulated debts.

The widow's appeal sounded like Hezekiah's and implied that she deserved something better if only because of her husband's faithful service to the Lord when he was alive. "Your servant my husband is dead, and you know that your servant feared the Lord," implying that she was willing to stand on his faithful service record.

Jewish historian Josephus identified this woman as the widow of the prophet Obadiah, who served in Ahab's court. He hid 100 of God's prophets in two caves, fifty to each cave. Then he kept them alive by bringing them provisions of bread and water from the king's kitchen. That would have required many trips each day. Imagine sneaking loaves and water out of the royal cupboard each day several times a day and doing it unnoticed.

His widow now implied that she deserved better than to lose her two sons to a creditor if only for her husband's faithful service. Her prayer sounded demanding.

Hezekiah stated his case just as boldly. "Remember now, O Lord, I pray, how I have walked before You in truth and with a loyal heart, and have done what was good in Your sight." And Hezekiah wept bitterly. What brought out this response was the prophet Isaiah's message from the Lord to Hezekiah to put his house in order because he would not survive his illness. There was no doubt about the message: "for you shall die, and not live."

Nehemiah, too, did not hesitate to speak a word on his own behalf. "Remember me, my God, for good, according to all that I have done for the people." And again later, he prayed, "Remember me, O my God, concerning this, and do not wipe out my good deeds that I have done for the house of my God, and for its services."

We might hesitate to shamelessly pray such prayers of entitlement, and with such boldness, but those three didn't. Desperate circumstances produce desperate prayers. How did God answer them?

Nehemiah prayed his prayer after showing fairness and benevolence to God's people and bringing reform to their worship and lifestyle practices. The widow's flask of oil, the only thing she had, was multiplied into many empty jars she had borrowed at Elisha's direction, and she sold all of it to pay all of her debts and have some left over to live on. Hezekiah's life was extended fifteen years when God directed Isaiah to return to the king to deliver a second message. "I have heard your prayer. I have seen your tears; surely I will heal you."

Is _that_ in the Bible?

Yes – in 1 Kings 18:3-4; 2 Kings 4:1, 20:1-3; Nehemiah 5:19, 13:14.

Does God ever change His mind?

God changed His mind in response to Hezekiah's prayer of entitlement and his bitter weeping. And he did it in a moment. But did He not also say, "I am the Lord, I do not change"? Indeed He did. He is the same yesterday, today and forever. His righteous nature never changes.

God's righteousness and unchangeable nature of love are not compromised by his attribute of mercy. He many times sent messages of judgment but cancelled or delayed them to another generation when the person or nation for whom the judgment was intended repented. God says He loves to show mercy. "I will show mercy to anyone I choose, and I will show compassion to anyone I choose."

He commissioned Jonah to bring a message of judgment to the city of Nineveh but it repented. No judgment. When wicked king Manasseh was carried off into captivity to Babylon, he implored the Lord in his affliction and God received his entreaty, heard his supplication and brought him back to Jerusalem into his kingdom. Then Manasseh knew that the Lord was God.

God, who is rich in mercy, consistently delayed or cancelled judgment in response to repentance because He loves to show mercy.

Is *that* in the Bible?

Yes – in Exodus 33:19; 2 Kings 20:1-3; 2 Chronicles 33:11-13; Malachi 3:6; Ephesians 2:4; Hebrews 13:8.

Why did Elisha direct the widow to close the door?

In response to the widow's request for help, Elisha asked her what she had in her home. "Nothing," she replied dismally, "except a jar of oil."

Elisha then directed her to borrow all the empty jars she could, not just a few. Then she was to close the door behind her and with her two sons pour her jar of oil into all the empty jars. A miracle was in the making and Elisha wanted to shield her. But from what? From prying eyes? From critical comments that might discourage her? Why was she to shut the door?

We might get an understanding from Jesus' own action in sending everyone outside the house when he was about raise Jairus' daughter from the dead. Doubt will neutralize faith so Jesus sent the people out. They had already demonstrated their attitude in ridiculing him when he said that the little girl was only asleep. Clearly not a very believing audience. Jesus knew they had to leave for he understood how effectively doubt can cancel faith.

When he came to his own home town one day, he went to the synagogue to teach but the people were offended because they knew who he was. This prompted Jesus to say that a prophet is not without honor except in his own country, among his own relatives. And he could do no mighty work there because of the people's unbelief.

No wonder he sent the unbelieving people out of the house allowing only Jairus and his wife and his three close disciples. Elisha may have understood this about miracles and the risks of ministry, so that in setting the widow up for a miracle, he admonished her to do all that he directed her to do but behind closed doors.

Is *that* in the Bible?

Yes – in 2 Kings 4:1-7; Mark 5:37-43, 6:1-6

Was Moses translated?
Joseph Quiambao

Both Moses and Elijah appeared in the New Testament. We know that Elijah had gone up into heaven by a whirlwind. But what about Moses?

A brief reference in the book of Jude indicates that Michael the archangel contended with the devil in disputing about the body of Moses. Moses had died in the land of Moab according to the word of the Lord. The Lord then buried him in a valley opposite Beth Peor.

Later (in the New Testament account), Moses appeared with Elijah in the Mount of Transfiguration. So Moses must have been resurrected and the Jude account of the disputing by the devil and Michael ended in the resurrection of Moses' body.

Is *that* in the Bible?

Yes – in Deuteronomy 34:5-6; 2 Kings 2:11; Matthew 17:3; Mark 9:4, Jude 9.

How did Jesus answer a challenge to His authority?

Miguel Ferrusquia

The leading priests and elders came up to Jesus and demanded "By what authority are you doing all these things?" And as a follow up, they asked "Who gave you the right?"

Jesus agreed to answer their question if they would answer one question. Jesus wasn't sidestepping anything. He was conforming to the custom of public discussions by responding to a question with another question, the answer to which would provide insight to the original question's answer. Jesus' authority to act came from God and He was eager for them to know that, but He also knew that they had rejected this authority in the case of John the Baptist, whose authority also came from God.

So Jesus' question was "Did John's authority to baptize come from heaven, or was it merely human?"

It was classic Jewish exchange in public debate and the priests and elders talked it among themselves. They realized the tight spot they were in because if they answered "from heaven" they knew He would ask why they didn't believe John. They also knew that if they answered "it was merely human" they would be mobbed because the people believed John was a prophet. They took the easy way out.

"We don't know," they finally replied.

Jesus responded, "Then I won't tell you by what authority I do these things." Case closed, by Jesus' conformity to public debate practice of their day.

In another incident, Jesus posed the question about the Messiah, "Whose son is he?" The Pharisees correctly answered "He is the son of David."

So Jesus asked "Then why does David, speaking under the inspiration of the Spirit, call the Messiah 'my Lord'? For

David said, 'The Lord said to my Lord, Sit in the place of honor at my right hand until I humble your enemies beneath your feet.' Since David called the Messiah 'my Lord,' how can the Messiah be his son?"

Clearly a conundrum to the Pharisees, and they could not answer Jesus. And the record says that no one dared to ask Him any more questions.

Is _that_ in the Bible?

Yes – in Matthew 21:23-27; 22:41-46.

What happened at Marah?
Gloria Williams

The name Marah meant "bitter" and referred to the bitter taste of the water in the oasis of Marah. It was rendered even more bitter by the lengthy three-day search for water in the desert before their disappointing discovery of the bitter waters so shortly after their magnificent deliverance through the Red Sea.

To cure the water of bitterness, the Lord showed Moses a piece of wood. Moses threw it into the water and this made it good to drink.

It was also there at Marah that the Lord set before His people a decree as a standard to test their faithfulness to Him. He said, "If you will listen carefully to the voice of the Lord your God and do what is right in His sight, obeying His commands and keeping all His decrees, then I will not make you suffer any of the diseases I sent on the Egyptians; for I am the Lord who heals you."

Is *that* in the Bible?

Yes – in Exodus 15:22-26
Note: The name of the Lord who heals is Yahweh-Rapha.

What was Jesus' prescription for being exalted?
Anjaan Shrestha

Humility.

He said "The greatest among you must be a servant. But those who exalt themselves will be humbled, and those who humble themselves will be exalted."

Peter, who had his share of experiences learning this principle, would write about this prescription years later in his epistle. He urged the younger people to submit themselves to their elders and for all to have the spirit of submissiveness to one another and to be clothed with humility. Then, quoting from Proverbs, he added "for God resists the proud and gives grace to the humble."

He concluded with "Therefore humble yourselves under the mighty hand of God, that He may exalt you in due time."

Jesus demonstrated it in His own life, humbling Himself even to the point of death on the cross. Therefore God also has highly exalted Him.

Is *that* in the Bible?

Yes – in Psalm 147:6; Proverbs 3:34; Matthew 23:11-12; Luke 18:14; Philippians 2:7-9; James 4:10; 1 Peter 5:5-6

What was Solomon's prescription for building a house?

Nellie Rizo

The wisest man who ever lived provided many directions for maintaining health, common sense living, or obtaining prosperity, among other popular topics. He said the proper sequence for building one's house was to first prepare your outside work, make it fit for yourself in the field; and afterward build your house.

A well-known paraphrase makes it clearer: Develop your business first before building your house. He is saying, given the same amount of investment capital, it is wiser to put your money to work first to produce a cash flow because it would continue to work for you in providing a cash flow even after you allocate part of that cash flow to build your house.

Is _that_ in the Bible?

Yes – in Proverbs 24:27. The paraphrase is taken from The Living Bible.

Why could the altar stones not be shaped by a tool?

Dake M. Deere

Only natural, uncut stones could be used to build an altar. That Israel's altars would not be like the Canaanites', these prohibitions were enacted and enforced. God said that using a tool to shape the altar stones would make the altar unfit for holy use.

Is *that* in the Bible?

Yes – in Exodus 20:25-26; Deuteronomy 27:5-6

Whose son was Zechariah?
Genalin Lopez

The minor prophet Zechariah was the son of Berechiah. Another prophet by the same name, but the son of Jehoiada, was stoned to death in the court of the house of the Lord during King Josiah's reign.

It was this Zechariah to whom Jesus was referring when He said that the nation would be responsible for the murder of all godly people of all time – from the murder of righteous Abel to the murder of Zechariah son of Berechiah (sic), who was killed in the Temple between the sanctuary and the altar at King Josiah's command. His tragic death seemed like unjust and terrible reward for the blessing that the priest's father Jehoiada had been to King Josiah. As he lay dying, he called on the Lord to "look on it, and repay."

It was this Zechariah to whom Jesus was referring. The scribe who copied this narrative may have mistakenly substituted the well-known name of Berechiah for Jehoiada as Zechariah's father.

Is *that* in the Bible?

Yes – in 2 Chronicles 24:15-22; Zechariah 1:1; Matthew 23:34-36; Luke 11:51.

Note: This prophecy and judgment spoken against the current generation of Jesus' time was fulfilled in AD 70 with the destruction of Jerusalem.

How is Jesus referred to after Calvary?

Ferry Rosos

In the gospels, Jesus is called the Son of God and He refers to Himself as the Son of Man. Sent by the Father He became the Incarnate Word (God who was made flesh). Despised and jeered, He bore the epithet of "Samaritan."

His perfect life and triumph over death enabled us to become adopted into God's family. After the gospels to the end of the Bible, Jesus acquires a new name. He went from Only Begotten Son of God to first born. As our Elder Brother, Jesus has made all of us His brothers and sisters, members of the family of God.

Is *That* in the Bible?

Yes – in Romans 8:29; Colossians 1:15, 18; Hebrews 1:6; Revelations 1:5

How and Why did Jesus become our Kinsman-Redeemer?

John D. Deeke

Only a kinsman could redeem a relative's property on behalf of that relative. In order for God to redeem man, He had first to become related to man. In a magnificent display of absolutely outlandish love, the Creator became related to the created when Jesus became a man.

By becoming related to us, He made it possible for us to be adopted into God's family. Through that adoption, we become eligible to receive the privileges of being family members, including receiving an inheritance; indeed, we have received an inheritance from God.

As man, He had the same weaknesses and was subject to the same temptations as we. He became one of us and, to use the expression the time and culture, He tabernacled (lived) among us.

His identity with us made Him our Kinsman, and His perfect life and triumph over death qualified Him to redeem us. O wondrous love!

Is _that_ in the Bible?

Yes – in Ephesians 1:5,11.

Is a leader guilty if he sins unknowingly?
Charlow Dedicatoria

If one of Israel's leaders sins by violating one of the commands of the Lord his God but doesn't realize it, he is still guilty. Ignorance of the commandment would not be acceptable excuse. When that person becomes aware of his sin, he must bring the specified offering.

The principle applied not only to the leaders but also to the common people. The difference was in the offerings: the leader's offering was to be a male goat with no defects and the people's offering a female goat with no defects.

Is _that_ in the Bible?

Yes – in Leviticus 4:22-23; 27-28

What is blasphemy against the Holy Spirit?
Mickie Hall

God had said "Woe to those who call evil good and good evil." That principle is behind the answer to this question.

The people had accused Jesus of having a demon and ascribed His miracle working power to Beelzebub. "By the ruler of the demons He casts out demons," they explained.

Jesus called these scribes and the people to Himself and through parables explained that Satan cannot cast out Satan and a house divided against itself cannot stand. Having made that point understood, Jesus now cautioned his audience to be careful about ascribing His works, which were done under the power of the Holy Spirit, to Satan. To do so would be blasphemous. He warned, "He who blasphemes against the Holy Spirit never has forgiveness but is subject to eternal condemnation." The next verse explains: because they said, "He has an unclean spirit" (thereby ascribing the works of the Holy Spirit to Satan).

Is *that* in the Bible?

Yes – in Isaiah 5:20; Matthew 9:34; Mark 3:20-30

Why did the high priest accuse Jesus of blasphemy?

Jesus replied to the high priest's query "Are You the Christ [the Greek word for Messiah]?" by saying "I am. And you will see the Son of Man sitting at the right hand of the Power and coming with the clouds of heaven."

The term "coming with the clouds of heaven" was associated with judgment. Jesus would someday sit in judgment and the people would stand on trial before him. This term juxtaposed to "sitting at the right hand of the Power" was simply too much for the high priest, who understood Jesus' answer to be a claim that He was God. Tearing his robe in mock horror and dismay, he said "What further need do we have of witnesses? You have heard the blasphemy!"

The tearing of his robe was a sign of great disrespect for his office.

Is _that_ in the Bible?

Yes – in Mark 14:62-64, Luke 22:67-70

At what point did the loaves and fish multiply?
Redeem Ebora

After hours of teaching ("the day was far spent"), Jesus directed His disciples to feed the multitude. Told that there was no food except for a few loaves and fishes, He asked that they be brought to Him and directed the disciples to have the people seated by groups of hundreds and fifties.

The loaf was a small roll (easier to imagine if you remember that it was from a boy's sack lunch). Jesus took the rolls and broke them, looked up into heaven and blessed the food.

The record says that Jesus blessed the food, broke the loaves and gave them to His disciples to set before the people. He must also have broken the fish because it says that Jesus divided the two fish among all His disciples. When He was done blessing the loaves, Jesus broke them and gave the pieces to His disciples. But the loaves did not multiply in Jesus' hands.

After He gave them the broken loaves and fish, the disciples distributed the food to the people. It was in the hands of the disciples that the food multiplied. Jesus performed the miracle and it was carried out in His disciples' hands.

Is _that_ in the Bible?

Yes – in Matthew 14:13-21; Mark 6:34-42; Luke 9:10-17.

How many did Jesus feed?
Glory S. Nytogaard

In one instance, Jesus feed 5,000, and in another it was 4,000. But that was the male count only.

In the culture of the day, only males were numbered. But there were women and children in both stories. Adjusting for an average number of women and children per male, the usual estimate given is about 15,000 in the feeding of the five thousand. Similar adjustments would be made for all census, including the number who left Egypt.

Is _that_ in the Bible?

Yes – in Mark 6:44; 8:9;

[Note: the feeding of the 5,000 is the only miracle recorded by all four gospel writers. After the miracle as recorded by John, Jesus delivered the sermon declaring Himself to be "the Bread of life." John 6:22-71]

What was the significance of the leftovers?

Asyll Saberola

Jesus modeled the virtue of conservation and told His disciples to gather up the fragments in both miracles of feeding, first the 5,000 and then the 4,000, "so that nothing is lost." But was there a significance to the number of baskets of leftovers? In the first miracle there were twelve baskets full and in the second, seven.

The number 12 was significant to the Jews as was the number 7 to Rome (which was built on 7 hills). The order of the miracles positioned twelve baskets being gathered after the feeding of the 5,000, before the seven baskets in the miracle of feeding the 4,000. This calls to mind that Jesus sent His disciples to go to the lost house of Israel first before going outside Israel, "into all the world."

Is _that_ in the Bible?

Yes – in Matthew 10:6, 14:20, 15:37, 28:19; Mark 6:53, 8:8, 16:15; Luke 9:6, John 6:12.

Whom only could a priest marry?

Dake M. Deere

A virgin.

Although it was allowed for the people to marry a widow, divorcee or a prostitute, priests were held to a higher standard of holiness.

Is *that* in the Bible?

Yes – in Leviticus 21:13, 15.

What were the consequences to the Levites who had abandoned their duty?

Homer Mendoza

Continuing to hold His servants the priests and Levites to a higher standard, God said that those Levites who had abandoned God by not keeping Israel from straying to worship idols (even taking part in encouraging idol worship) would have to bear the consequences: they could no longer approach the Lord on behalf of the people or to minister as priests. Their duties would be reduced to being temple guards and gatekeepers and to slaughtering the animals brought for burnt offerings, serving as caretakers, taking charge of the maintenance work and performing general duties.

The exception would be the Levitical priests of the family of Zadok who would continue to stand in the Lord's presence and approach His table to serve Him, because they continued to minister faithfully in the temple and did not encourage Israel to worship idols during the period when Israel abandoned God for idols.

Is *that* in the Bible?

Yes – in Ezekiel 44:10-16.

Why were the priests to change clothes when returning to the outer courtyard?

Melissa Tanap

The priests put on special clothes, set apart as holy, while ministering to the Lord in the sanctuary. Upon the conclusion of their duty and before returning to the courtyard, they were to change clothes, leaving their ceremonial robes in the sacred rooms. This was a precaution because holiness is transmitted through holy things, and transmitting holiness to the people through the holy clothing would endanger the people. In His instructions to Israel through Moses, God said that touching the holy objects of the sanctuary would cause people to die.

Is _that_ in the Bible?

Yes – in Exodus 29:29, 30:29, 31:10, 35:19, 39:41; Numbers 4:15; Ezekiel 44:17-19

What was done to the meat and bread that were left over from the offerings of ordination?

Michelle Yanez

They were burned. They were not to be eaten because it was holy.

Is _that_ in the Bible?

Yes – in Exodus 29:29, 34; Leviticus 8:31-32

Note: Even today (in some churches), the elements of Grace left over from communion are similarly disposed of by burning.

When did Jesus say No to a request for discipleship?

Vancine Wilson

When the demoniac (two in the Matthew account) asked to follow Jesus.

Jesus had sought some rest from ministry and had come to the other side of the sea to the country of the Gadarenes. Immediately He was met by a man with an unclean spirit who had been cutting himself with stones and had broken all shackles and chains placed on him.

Jesus set the man free and when people saw him sitting, clothed and in his right mind, they were afraid. Meanwhile, the residents begged Jesus to leave because of the frightening sequence of events that saw a herd of 2000 swine, entered by the demons Jesus cast out of the demoniac, drown in the sea.

As Jesus was getting ready to leave, the former demoniac begged if he might be with Him. Jesus did not permit him. Instead, He urged him to go home to tell his family and friends what great things the Lord did for him. His witness caused people to marvel.

The man's commissioning was based on his encounter with Jesus, not on the training that he sought as a follower of Jesus. The seeds sown from his witness bore much fruit. When Jesus arrived in Decapolis later, a whole city was ready to receive Him as a result of that witness.

Is _that_ in the Bible?

Yes – in Matthew 8:28-34; Mark 5:1-20; Luke 8:26-36; Mark 7:31

What is the opposite of "fear"?
Jismar Abquilan

Jesus was asleep in the stern of a boat that was being buffeted by the winds and waves. Awakened by His disciples, He rebuked the wind and said to the sea, "Peace, be still!" Then turning to His disciples, He asked "Why are you so fearful? How is it that you have no faith?"

In another incident, Jesus was walking with Jairus in the direction of Jairus' home. Jairus' daughter was at the point of death and Jesus had agreed to the request to come lay His hands on her that she might be healed.

On the way there, someone from Jairus' household arrived to inform him that his daughter had died, and not to trouble the Teacher any further. To encourage Jairus, Jesus said "Do not be afraid; only believe."

In both cases, Jesus identified the opposite of "fear." He said it was "faith" or "belief."

Is _that_ in the Bible?

Yes – in Mark 4:40; 5:36

What is "mystery"?
Marie Aleli C. Haboc

The term "mystery" means something formerly hidden but now revealed. It also cannot be understood except by divine revelation. The secret thoughts, plans and dispensations of God remain hidden from unregenerate mankind, but are revealed to all believers. This is what Jesus explained to His disciples when they asked Him "Why do you speak in parables?"

His answer quoted Isaiah, "Seeing they may see and not perceive, and hearing they may hear and not understand."

This mystery which has been hidden for ages and from generations, has now been revealed to His saints: Christ's sinless life, atoning death, powerful resurrection, and dynamic ascension.

Is _that_ in the Bible?

Yes – in Isaiah 6:9-10; Mark 4:11; Colossians 1:26

What did David do when his men threatened to stone him?
Alma Lou Fordek

Among the men who made up David's band were those who were in distress, in debt or were discontented. It isn't hard then to imagine that these malcontents could conspire against David if the circumstances so provoked them.

And there was such a circumstance when the Amalekites attacked Ziklag where David and his men had set up camp. They were gone for some time and in their absence the Amalekites invaded the area and took captive all who were there, not killing anyone but carrying them away. When David and his men found the place burned and with their families gone, they lifted up their voices and wept until they had no more power to weep. The disgruntled men then spoke of stoning David because of their great distress.

But David's response was not to bow to fear but to encourage himself in the Lord, to strengthen himself in the Lord God. He then inquired of the Lord who told him to pursue and that he would overtake the enemy and recover all without the loss of one.

Is _that_ in the Bible?

Yes – in 1 Samuel 22:1-2, 30:1-9

What does it mean to dare to be a Daniel?

Rey S. Puson

The well-known song of an older generation refers to standing firmly for principle, as Daniel and his three friends did (as when Daniel purposed in his heart not to defile himself with a portion of the king's delicacies or wine, or his three friends' refusal to bow before the king's statue, even on the penalty of being thrown into the fiery furnace).

Note also the fabric of Daniel's character in his determination to stem the king's anger in ordering all the wise men of the kingdom (those appointed to interpret times or provide political leadership) to be killed. Daniel went in to the king and asked him for more time, and then with his three friends Hananiah, Mishael and Azariah, sought the Lord in prayer. He had the confidence to ask the king for time because he also had the confidence to go to the Lord for help.

God rewarded that confidence and gave Daniel both the king's dream and its interpretation in a night vision.

Is _that_ in the Bible?

Yes – in Daniel 2-3

What is the message in Daniel's friends' faithfulness?
Migy T. Reswand

Satan as the god of this age seeks to draw men's attention to the spirit of this world and, through their fixation on it, seduce them into bowing to images designed to draw them away from their loyalty to the true God. These images make up our idols – anything that comes between us and God or comes before God.

Jesus' appearance in the fiery furnace reminds us of His commitment to be with us to resist the plans and tactics of the enemy. Whether He appears visibly or invisibly, He is there to strengthen us to meet any conflict and to encourage and protect those who suffer for their steadfastness and testimony.

The fourth man was a pre-incarnate appearance of Jesus whom even Nebuchadnezzar recognized to be like the Son of God. Jesus' commitment to never abandon us will come into play again in the end time events.

Is _that_ in the Bible?

Yes – in Daniel 3; 2 Corinthians 4:4

What should a high priest never do with his clothing?

God specified that the high priest should not uncover his head (an act of mourning) or tear his clothes. At Jesus' trial, Caiaphas tore his clothes in violation of this instruction in mock horror at Jesus' blasphemy.

Is _that_ in the Bible?

Yes – in Leviticus 21:10; Matthew 26:57, 65.

Why did soldiers fall at Jesus' feet?

Jesus was sensitive to His Father's agenda, many times reminding others that His time had not yet come. He was referring to the time when He would be offered up as a sacrifice, the purpose for His descent to earth to pay for man's sin as the Passover Lamb.

Finally, His time had come. He knew before the Feast of the Passover that the hour had come that He should depart from this world to the Father. He said "Father, the hour has come. Glorify Your Son, that Your Son also may glorify You."

So on His way to being arrested, Jesus was with His disciples in the Garden of Gethsemane where He had spent the night in prayer. Judas knew the place well because it was a favorite place where Jesus used to spend tie with His disciples. Judas had agreed to betray his master for 30 pieces of silver and led a detachment of troops to arrest Jesus.

Jesus did not shirk from meeting his appointed time. He came forward and asked "Whom are you seeking?" They answered, "Jesus of Nazareth." The name Jesus was a common one and, as with other similar common names, anyone with that name was further identified by his hometown. When Jesus said "I am *He*" the people drew back and fell to the ground.

Throughout scripture, italicized words indicate that they don't appear in the original but are supplied in order to make the translation make sense in English. The word *He* is italicized, indicating that Jesus just replied "I am." He wasn't the only one who spoke that way.

The man born blind from birth, after washing in the pool of Siloam at Jesus' direction, came back seeing. People exclaimed, "Isn't this the one who sat and begged?" The people were divided, some saying "This is he," and others saying "He is like him." So the formerly blind man settled it and said "I am *he*." Again, the word is italicized, meaning he said "I am." It must have been a manner and pattern of speech of the culture to simply say "I am", omitting the nominative case personal pronoun "*he.*"

But for Jesus, I AM was also His divine name. When Moses asked who he should tell the Israelites was sending him to them, God answered "I AM WHO I AM." Moses was to tell the children of Israel, "I AM has sent me to you." This divine name declares His character and attributes, implying in the original Hebrew the absolute existence of God.

And now responding to the soldiers' search for Jesus of Nazareth, He admitted to being the one they were looking for – "I AM." When he said that, He also uttered His divine name. There was a momentary unleashing of His inherent power as God and the troops were smitten by that power, however briefly.

That's why they drew back and fell to the ground.

Is *that* in the Bible?

Yes – in Ex. 3:13-14; Matt. 26:14-16; John 9:9; 13:1; 17:1; 18:1-6.

What were God's instructions regarding tattoos?

Evonne Williams

People were not to mark their skin with tattoos.

Marking their bodies was part of the worship ritual of pagan deities. In one memorable incident to demonstrate who the true God was, Elijah challenged Baal's priests to cry out to their god to accept their offerings by burning them. They did, but to no avail. Their altar's sacrifice went unburned. In a desperate act to get the attention of their god (whom Elijah mocked as meditating or too busy or on a journey or sleeping), Baal's priests cut themselves as was their worship custom.

Is _that_ in the Bible?

Yes – in Leviticus 19:28; Deuteronomy 14:1; 1 Kings 18:22-40

What was Jesus' last miracle?

Ever obedient to His Father's timetable, Jesus went to the Garden of Gethsemane in His appointment with destiny. Judas found Him there, having led a detachment of troops and officers from the chief priests and Pharisees, all carrying lanterns, torches and weapons. It was night.

When Jesus offered himself up without resistance, one disciple decided to take matters into his hands and put up a fight. Peter drew his sword and cut off the high priest's servant's ear. His name was Malchus.

Jesus admonished him to put his sword in its place for all who take the sword will perish by the sword. He then asked, rhetorically, "How then could the scriptures be fulfilled, that it must happen thus?"

So Jesus reached out and touched Malchus' ear and healed it. Being surrounded by those who arrested him and were taking him to judgment, it would be Jesus' last opportunity to perform a miracle of healing.

Is *that* in the Bible?

Yes – in Matthew 26:52; Luke 22:51; John 18:10-11.

Why did God promise a triple harvest in the sixth year of every seven-year cycle?

God directed Israel to allow the land to lie fallow each seventh year. Today, agriculturists understand this to be the best cycle by which to allow the land to be renewed through its rest. This would parallel the Sabbath-day principle God had laid for Israel, to do no work on each seventh day of the week.

Because there would be no harvest in the seventh year, God made provision for this lack by giving the land a triple harvest on the sixth year. This way the people would have food for the current and next two years (the triple harvest covered the sixth year, the seventh year, and through the first year of the new cycle before the produce of that year could be brought in).

Did the harvest keep for three years? That was part of the continuing miracle.

Is *that* in the Bible?

Yes – in Leviticus 25:18-22.

What was the Jubilee?

God commanded that the land was to rest every seventh year. There was to be no planting or harvesting, although the people and their livestock and wild animals could eat of the produce of the ground. After seven seventh years (49), there would be a celebration in the following year – the fiftieth – which was called the Year of Jubilee. It would be a time of great rejoicing and a year-long celebration. People would be allowed to receive back the original land that had been apportioned to their ancestors. Any debt with it as collateral would be cancelled and the land would revert to the original owner free and clear.

This property would have been sold if an Israelite fell into poverty. It would be somewhat like our taking out a loan against our property, except that the terms the Israelites had were more favorable. They could buy it back for less because what they were "renting" out was the land's harvests. Therefore the cost of redemption would drop each year because of the diminishing number of harvests.

God warned the people not to take advantage of each other. The price was determined by the number of years since the last Jubilee. Then on the Year of Jubilee, the land title would revert back to the original owners.

It was a year in which the land was not to be planted, making it two years in a row that the land was allowed to lie fallow (seven sevens is 49, which would be the year immediately before the Year of Jubilee which, being a seventh year, would also be a year the land lay fallow). Because the land would become free of any encumbrances, the Jubilee year was a time to proclaim freedom throughout the land and was a time for great rejoicing.

Is _that_ in the Bible?

Yes – in Leviticus 25:1-38

What was the law about gleaning?
Generis L. Avafada

God wanted His people to develop compassion for the poor. He provided for them partly through a law about gleaning that would allow the poor to follow after the reapers to pick what had been left over, dropped, or in the corners of the field. Not every grape in a vineyard should be gleaned, but some left for the poor and the stranger.

Ruth the Moabitess went to glean heads of grain from Boaz' field. Boaz assured her that she would be safe there and admonished his workers to purposely let grain fall from their bundles for her to glean. This beautiful narrative that develops into a wonderful love story (see the entry on Kinsman-Redeemer) started with Ruth's gleaning in Boaz' field.

Is _that_ in the Bible?

Yes – in Leviticus 19:9-10; Ruth 2

What was a Kinsman-Redeemer?
Dake M. Deere

God had specified that the land could not be sold on a permanent basis, explaining that it was because "the land belongs to Me." Instead of obtaining a loan against the land as we might do today, the owner would sell the property, knowing that there was provision for its eventual return.

177

One was during the Year of Jubilee when freedom from all debts would be proclaimed throughout the land.

The other was through repurchase at any time before the Year of Jubilee. God directed that with every purchase of land, a buyer must grant the seller the right to buy it back. If that seller saved enough money to buy it back, he could exercise that privilege and it would always be at a discount – the discount size depending on the number of years left to the next Jubilee.

If the seller didn't have enough money to buy his land back, he or his descendants could always wait until the next Jubilee. Or the land could be redeemed. (The act of buying the land back was redeeming it.) But who could do that?

Only a close relative could. Because of his ability and willingness to redeem the land to keep it in the family, he was called a Kinsman-Redeemer. There could be any number of Kinsmen-Redeemer and a strict order of succession was followed. If the closest Kinsman-Redeemer chose to pass, the next in line could step up.

Boaz was one such Kinsman-Redeemer. He stepped in as a relative who qualified to redeem the land that had been sold by Elimelech. Although he wasn't the closest relative, he obtained that privilege by default when the closest Kinsman-Redeemer declined to exercise the Kinsman-Redeemer privilege. Boaz was eager to step into the role as the next Kinsman-Redeemer in line because there was an additional agenda he had in mind (a woman was involved). You can read the rest of this story in the book of Ruth which contains an example of the rules of inheritance and land redemption.

Besides, it's a wonderful love story.

Is *that* in the Bible?

Yes – in Leviticus 25:23-28; Ruth 4:1-12.

What did the Kinsman redeem and why?
May Grace Sisfurva

A good substitute for kinsman-redeemer is "relative." But the English language has no equivalent for the concept of obligation of a family member toward another relative who has suffered loss. This concept is a cultural one and most strongly experienced in third-world countries.

It involves the capacity of one relative who may be qualified to redeem another relative from being a slave or to recover property lost because of indebtedness.

Is *that* in the Bible?

Yes – in Leviticus 25:25, 47-55

Why did Ruth lie down at the foot of Boaz' bed?
Peter L. Giespy

Naomi's instructions and Ruth's obedient action may appear to be seductive and incongruent to the book's spiritual nobility. What Naomi had directed Ruth to do was to wash herself and anoint herself (put on perfume). Then to dress herself in the best dress she had and go down to the threshing floor, but to avoid making herself known to Boaz until after he was done with his meal.

Then after he was to lie down, she was to mark the spot, move in softly, take the sheet off to uncover his feet, and lie down. Then she was to expect him to tell her what to do.

He did just that, assuring her of his interest in her, but that there was a small impediment – another relative was a closer relative than he. However, that impediment would soon be managed.

Is *that* in the Bible?

Yes – in Ruth 3:3-14

Why did the other relative pass up the privilege of redemption?
Priscilla Shrestha

The prerogative of exercising the kinsman-redeemer role belonged to a relative closer to Ruth than Boaz. Boaz was determined to set the wheels in motion that would allow that relative to exercise his privilege or by passing it up allow it to pass on to Boaz who would exercise it.

He convened ten elders of the city at the city gate – the usual place for transacting official business. The other relative already was there.

Boaz set the stage in front of the elders as witnesses, that Naomi had returned from Moab, had earlier sold the piece of land which belonged to her husband Elimelech, related to both Boaz and this "closer" relative. Boaz asked this relative to exercise his right to redeem it or if he passed it up, Boaz as next in line would exercise it.

The relative agreed to redeem it but changed his mind when he realized he also had to receive Ruth in order to

Is *that* in the Bible?

Yes – in Ruth 4:1-12

Why did God choose 70 years as the length of Israel's captivity?

(The term "Israel" or "children of Israel" is used here and in other portions of the Bible as representing God's chosen people, whether from the northern kingdom of Israel or the southern kingdom of Judah.)

Israel had been repeatedly warned by the prophets that they would be carried off into captivity for their disobedience of the Lord's commandments by their idolatry. But they never responded to the warnings with repentance and permanent turning away from idolatry. So they were carried into exile. When that happened, the number fixed for their term of exile was 70 years. Why?

The people had also disobeyed God's command to let the land lie fallow each seventh year. By God's accounting, there must have been 490 years during which the land's Sabbath rest had been denied. To correct this, the length of the exile was fixed to be exactly the number of years that the land had been denied its rest. Thus during their exile, the people effectively abandoned their land and in so doing allowed the books to be balanced with regard to this commandment.

Is _that_ in the Bible?

Yes – in Leviticus 25:43 and 2 Chronicles 36:20-21.

How was Nehemiah made dreadfully fearful by the King's question?

Nehemiah was a favored staff member in King Artaxerxes' court, serving the king as his personal cupbearer. One of the duties of the cupbearer was to taste the wine to make sure that it wasn't poisoned, before serving it to the king.

Nehemiah had won great favor with the king and this would be demonstrated by the king's giving him permission to return to Judah to repair the walls which had fallen into disrepair. The king also gave him letters authorizing the providing of timber from the king's forest, and gave him captains of the army and horsemen to accompany Nehemiah and the volunteer workmen.

But the cause for this great concern Nehemiah carried in his heart was the report of the reproach and distress that the survivors of the captivity were suffering and the state of Jerusalem's broken-down walls. When Nebuchadnezzar had taken the people of Judah into captivity, a few escaped that capture and stayed home. But their lot was miserable and they suffered distressfully.

Nehemiah was burdened by this report. Unfortunately, he was so overtaken by sadness that he momentarily forgot the custom that he was not to reflect anything but cheer and a positive atmosphere in the king's presence. In fact, to do otherwise would reflect badly on the king and be taken as an insult and this was punishable by death.

Thus when Nehemiah went about his duties unaware that his sadness was reflected on his countenance and he heard the king ask "Why is your face sad since you're not sick?" Nehemiah was stricken with terror. He knew the penalty could be death and quickly offered the explanation for his sadness.

Nehemiah's many years of faithful service provided him favor with the king who proceeded to become a big part of the solution that Nehemiah sought.

Is _that_ in the Bible?

Yes – in Nehemiah 1 and 2.

How could Nehemiah lead the people to confess the sins of their fathers?

Nehemiah asked Persian King Artaxerxes whom he served as cupbearer for permission to go to Jerusalem to repair its broken-down walls. He was accompanied by several volunteers. After the walls were repaired but before their dedication, Nehemiah had Ezra read from the Book of the Law, and this was followed by a joyous celebration.

A few days later, Nehemiah assembled the people to confess their sins and the iniquities of their ancestors. Could they do that – confess someone else's iniquities? Yet that's what Nehemiah and Daniel did. They not only confessed their ancestors' iniquities but as intercessors, they identified with their ancestors even though they hadn't committed those specific sins being confessed. Intercessors often number themselves with transgressors. They could do that for iniquities, but not for sins. (Each one had to bear his own sin.)

And so in their hour of most urgent need, Nehemiah led the people in a time of confession, not only of their sins but also of their ancestors' iniquities.

Is _that_ in the Bible?

Yes – in Deuteronomy 24:16; Nehemiah 1:6, 8:1-12, 9:2; Exodus 34:7,9; Leviticus 26:46; Ezekiel 18:20; Daniel 9:5

How many generations did Abraham's iniquity touch?

The second commandment states that God would visit the iniquities of the fathers upon the children for four generations. God also said that fathers would not bear the guilt for their sons' sins, nor sons be punished for their fathers' sins. Each would bear his own punishment.

So what is the difference between sin and iniquity?

In context, the word *iniquity* is used to identify unconfessed sin. Its effects in one generation are then passed on to the next generation. So when Abraham asked his wife Sarah to tell a lie (because he was afraid that her beauty would cause some man to kill him) by telling anyone who asked that she was Abraham's sister, he set something in motion that can be traced for four generations.

Another characteristic of this occurrence is that the iniquity becomes more severe with each generation. When Abraham persuaded Sarah to tell a lie, it was only a white lie because she was his half-sister. Isaac's lie was almost a carbon copy of his father's lie, except that Rebekah wasn't his half-sister. It was an outright lie. Then Jacob came along and stole his father's blessing intended for Esau, and he told a bold-faced lie. He said "I am Esau." A generation later, Jacob's ten sons practiced intentional deception by dipping Joseph's coat of many colors in goat's blood and asked their father if he recognized the coat. Of course Jacob did. The iniquity (also identified as a stronghold) of deception had gone four generations, each occurrence more severe than in the previous generation.

Is *that* in the Bible?

Yes – in Genesis 12:10-13; 20:2, 5, 12; 26:6-7; 27:19; 37:31-32; Exodus 20:5; Deuteronomy 24:16; Ezekiel 18:20.

What's with extending the consequences of iniquity over four generations?

We may not fully understand this matter as God's ways are past finding out. He said that his ways are higher than our ways. We will always have questions that seem unanswered in scripture or life, except to know that God's ways are beyond our ability to comprehend them.

But one can be cheered to know that the extent of iniquity's judgment is limited to only four generations. This emphasis is contained in the definition of God's mercy. He loves to show mercy to thousands of generations but limits the effects of iniquity to only four generations.

This inclusion is contained in several passages where God speaks of His character. He told Moses that He could not allow him to see his face else he would die, but God would allow Moses to view His glory as He passed before him in the cleft of a rock. As He did so, God proclaimed "The Lord, the Lord God, merciful and gracious, long-suffering, and abounding in goodness and truth, keeping mercy for thousands, forgiving iniquity and transgression and sin, by no means clearing the guilty, visiting the iniquity of the fathers upon the children and the children's children to the third and the fourth generation."

Note that when God defined His mercy, He included the fact that He would limit the results of iniquity to only four generations. This inclusion is found in other passages defining the mercy of God. Thus while we may not be able to fully understand why others have to suffer for our iniquities or we for the iniquities of a previous generation, we are given to view a much wider vista – the wide mercy of God's love.

Is _that_ in the Bible?

Yes – in Exodus 20:5; 34:6-7; Isaiah 55:8-9; Jeremiah 31:34; 32:18; Romans 11:33.

Why did Jesus' disciples ask if a certain blind man might be suffering for his parents' sins?

The prevailing opinion throughout Bible times was that people suffered for their own sins and also for generational curses. That's why Nehemiah, Jehoshaphat, Daniel, and others, confessed corporate sins as a prelude to seeking God's divine favor, blessings, and direction.

Unconfessed sins in a previous generation would pass down as iniquities and become the basis for strongholds. (See the previous entry.)

Thus it was natural for Jesus' disciples as well as anyone during their time to assume that one suffering from blindness or other ailment may perhaps be suffering from a generational curse if not as a result of their own carelessness or sins.

Is _that_ in the Bible?

Yes – in Exodus 20:5; John 9:1-3

How did a certain funeral end up with the dead person being resurrected?

A news wire report in April 2006 describes the modern Taliban in Afghanistan as scheduling warfare in the spring according to their military custom. This modern-day military custom goes all the way back to Old Testament times when kings went to war after the crops had been planted. If marauding bands invaded the land in the spring, it would be when kings had gone out to battle.

One memorable incident happened during a funeral. Perhaps while still digging the grave, the funeral party spied a band of raiders. Intending perhaps to return later to complete the job, the men hurriedly put the dead man in a neighboring tomb. It happened to be the tomb of the prophet Elisha, whose life and ministry had been marked by miracles.

One more miracle remained from his body, even in death. When the dead man's body, being hurriedly let down, touched the bones of Elisha, the dead man revived and stood on his feet.

Is _that_ in the Bible?

Yes – in 2 Kings 13:20-21; 2 Samuel 11:1; 1 Kings 20:22, 26; 1 Chronicles 20:1-2; Chronicles 24:23.

Why is the death of His saints precious in the sight of the Lord?

God's people (sometimes referred to as *saints*) are always precious to Him because of the price paid by the death of his Son. But there is another dimension of value in the word *precious* in its original meaning.

That which is precious is treasured. For example, we use "precious" in connection with memories we treasure. But in this verse, the word "precious" means costly, as in precious metals. God's plan for our salvation was costly. It cost His only Son. In that same sense, there is something costly in the sight of the Lord. What is it?

It's the death of a saint.

That's one less intercessor, one less prayer warrior, one less gospel worker, one less witness for the truth. And that makes it an expensive and costly exchange. In the sight of the Lord, the death of a saint is costly. It is precious.

Is *that* in the Bible?

Yes – in Psalm 116:15.

What is the significance of the bride's marching down the aisle on her father's left arm?

The left side is the power side. Jesus sits at the right hand of God, so God is on the left side. The right side is the place of honor (NLT).

All the way down the aisle, and on the left arm of her father, the bride retains the power to change her mind. She goes down that walk under her old name. But unless she exercises her power to change her mind, she is about to surrender both name and position to the bridegroom soon to be her husband.

After the bride and groom publicly declare their vows and she takes on his name, they turn around to be introduced to the congregation, and a marvelous transformation takes place. Now he's on the left side! The power side! And she's on the right side, the place of honor! She comes under his authority. He is to love her as the Lord loves the church, and the symbolism remains intact: the new Christian abandons his old life, takes on a new name, and submits to a new authority. In a marriage, the wife takes the right side of honor, and it is on her that the husband bestows honor as she abandons her old name and takes on her husband's name.

Is *that* in the Bible?

Yes – in Romans 8:34; Ephesians 5:22, 24-25; Colossians 3:1, 18-19; Hebrews 12:2; 1 Peter 3:7.

In what Bible book is the name of God not mentioned?

The book of Esther is a significant book that tells of God's protection of the Jews and their survival in a world of hostility. The Feast of Purim was instituted to mark the Jews' magnificent deliverance in a series of plots and subplots that underscore God's watch care and orchestration of events to deliver His people.

Yet, though there is ample opportunity to mention God's name anywhere in those ten chapters, His name is omitted. Why?

Some Jewish sources offer this explanation: so that when the non-Jews of Ahasuerus' kingdom read the Megilla (the basis for Jewish celebration of Purim) they would not substitute the name of their own gods.

Though there is no mention of God's name, any reading of this book will uncover convincing evidence of a Higher Power at work. It may also be that the book, written in a foreign country where the name of God was not worshipped, may have intentionally omitted any reference that would result in banning the book's reading or distribution.

(Those who employ the Bible code software say that results of computer searches have yielded the mention of

God's name in several places under the Esther narrative. *You can find out more by googling "bible codes" or "equidistant letter spacing."*)

Is _that_ in the Bible?

Yes – In the book of Esther. The explanation is offered in various Jewish commentaries.

How can one be an Ephrathite from Bethlehem?

An Ephrathite is from the tribe of Ephraim and Bethlehem is in Judah. How can one be an Ephrathite from Bethlehem?

Bethlehem, five miles south of Jerusalem in Judah, takes on significance because it was identified with another tribe – Ephraim. David is described as an Ephrathite of Bethlehem. Elimelech, his wife Naomi, and sons Mahlon and Chilion, went to dwell in Moab during a time of famine. They were described as Ephrathites of Bethlehem.

How can a town in Judah belong to Ephraim? Because Rachel, Joseph's mother and Ephraim's grandmother, was buried there.

Before the Promised Land was divided among the 12 tribes, the place where Jacob's favored wife was buried, and its city, became a sacred spot to Joseph's line. Rachel's tomb there is still revered to this day, a mecca of hope to barren women. Thus, residents of Bethlehem, the place where Ephraim's grandmother was buried, were Ephrathites.

Was it necessary to identify them thus?

Yes, if there were two Bethlehems. And there were.

The other, less-known, one was in the northern most part of Israel, in the tribe of Zebulon. But the Bethlehem in Judah was the prophetic site. The prophet Micah addresses Bethlehem Ephrathah as little among the thousands of Judah, yet out of it would come the One to be Ruler in Israel.

When Jesus was born in Bethlehem, was He from Judah or Ephraim?

Both! Bethlehem didn't belong to Judah... but it was situated in Judah.

Residents there were Ephrathites.

Is *that* in the Bible?

Yes – in Genesis 35:19; Ruth 1:1-2; Joshua 10:10,15; 1 Samuel 17:12; and Micah 5:2

How many nails were used in the building of the Temple?

None.

The stone was finished at the quarry so that no hammer or chisel or any iron tool was heard in the temple while it was being built.

Is *that* in the Bible?

Yes – in 1 Kings 6:7

When was an elevator used in the Bible?

They didn't call it that but in at least two instances, people were transported down a window or opening in the city wall. In both instances, it was to facilitate an escape. (Another instance was when Jesus healed a paralytic whose stretcher was let down through the roof.)

When Joshua sent two spies to bring back a report about Jericho, they were hidden in the roof by stalks of flax covering them. Rahab used diversionary tactics to keep the king's messengers from inspecting her house, admitting that the spies had been there earlier but had left as the gates were being shut, and urging them to hurry out after them.

Then after the king's messengers left, Rahab went up to her rooftop and told the spies her conviction that the Lord had given them the land, and negotiated protection from them. She then let them down by a rope through the window, for her house was on the city wall.

When Paul was baptized by Ananias after a brief period in pursuit of Christians to persecute them, he immediately preached the Christ in the synagogues so that all who heard him were amazed, saying "Isn't this the same man who caused such devastation among Jesus' followers in Jerusalem?" Saul, as he was still known, became more and more powerful in his preaching so that the Jews couldn't refute his proofs that Jesus was indeed the Messiah. They then plotted to kill him, but Saul was told about their plot.

So during the night, some of the other believers lowered him in a large basket through an opening in the city wall.

Is *That* in the Bible?

Yes – in Joshua 2:5, 12-15; Mark 2:4; Acts 9:21-25.

Why did 50,070 men of Beth Shemesh die when they saw the ark?

The Philistine war had resulted in the death of Eli's two sons and the capture of the ark of God (1 Sam. 4). The Philistines took the ark and set it before their god Dagon in Ashdod. The next morning the people discovered Dagon fallen on its face to the earth before the ark, so they set Dagon in its place again.

The next morning, the statue had again fallen on its face but this time its head and both palms of its hands were broken, leaving only Dagon's torso. Tumors ravaged the Ashdod populace and the people decided to send the ark to Gath. The hand of God similarly smote the people there with great destruction and with tumors.

When the ark was sent to another Philistine city, Ekron, it was accompanied again by deadly destruction in the city. All who survived were stricken with tumors. The city leaders then decided to send the ark back to Israel and inquired of their priests and diviners how to do that. The answer was that it should be accompanied with a trespass offering of five golden tumors and five golden rats representing the number of Philistine lords. (Gaza and Ashkelon were the other two Philistine cities.)

"Why then," the Philistine lords were admonished, "would you harden your hearts as the Egyptians and Pharaoh hardened their hearts?" The events of more than 500 years earlier had not been forgotten even by the heathen nations.

A new cart was constructed and hitched to two milk cows which had never been yoked. The people knew that if the cows headed for Beth Shemesh, it was the Lord God of Israel who was behind this plague. Separated from their calves, the milk cows pulled the cart loaded with the ark of the Lord and a chest containing the trespass offerings.

The cows headed straight for Beth Shemesh just across the border into Israel.

The people of Beth Shemesh were reaping the wheat harvest in the valley and when they spotted the ark being returned, they broke out in rejoicing. The cart stopped in the field of Joshua and the Levites took down the ark and the chest and placed both on the large stone. The people split the wood of the cart and offered the cows as a burnt offering to the Lord.

Although the Hebrew construction creates some question as to the distribution of the 50,070 people (70 from Beth Shemesh and 50,000 from surrounding communities perhaps), they nevertheless were struck dead because they dared to look into the ark of the Lord. Under proper circumstances, people could view the ark, covered and carried on the shoulders of the Levites, without risk of death. The narrative says that they looked *into* the ark of the Lord. This may imply that they looked where they shouldn't have looked.

God had told Moses that no one could look on His face and live. Sinful man cannot survive the presence of a holy God. So God provided a mercy seat of pure gold to cover the top of the ark in which the two tables of stone containing the Ten Commandments were placed. The ark represented the holy presence of God and the Ten Commandments are a transcript of God's character of holiness. Being exposed to them without the lid of the mercy seat would result in the incineration of mortal man.

It may be that that's what happened in Beth Shemesh as the people peered into the ark out of curiosity and unprotected by the mercy seat.

Is *that* in the Bible?

Yes – in 1 Samuel 4-6 and 2 Samuel 6:1-7

Why did God kill Uzzah when he tried to steady the ark?

The ark of the Lord had been placed in the home of Abinadab after the unfortunate events at Beth Shemesh. His son Eleazar was consecrated to act as priest to take care of the ark of the Lord. There it remained for about 70 years until David became king and made arrangements for its transfer to Jerusalem.

No one was allowed to touch the ark, not even the priests. Although some may surmise that Uzzah was acting honorably in trying to steady the ark when the oxen stumbled, the Bible says that he was killed for his error (better translated "lack of reverence").

None of this would have been problematical had Israel followed God's instructions in the first place, to have the ark carried on the shoulders of the Levites.

Is _that_ in the Bible?

Yes - in Deuteronomy 10:8; 1 Chronicles 15:2; and 1 Samuel 7:1.

What was the law of the Medes and Persians?

It was a law that couldn't be commuted. Once enacted, it couldn't be withdrawn or altered (Dan. 6:8). It could only be offset by another law that would allow actions to counter the intended purpose of the previous law, as in the case of Queen Esther. Ahasuerus had agreed to Haman's devious proposal to exterminate a certain people he hinted were seditious and dangerous to the king's reign. The king signed the decree into law unwittingly, not knowing that he was condemning his queen Esther and the Jews to extermination, and sealed it with his signet ring.

Although such a law couldn't be changed, another law could be passed to counter the effect of the first law. This was the case with the law passed to destroy the Jews in Queen Esther's day. The wicked Haman was the force behind this evil plan and even when he was overthrown, the law which he had engineered was still in effect.

So another law was drafted and sent to all the provinces in the kingdom, allowing the Jews to defend themselves with weapons. The first law couldn't be changed, but the second law effectively neutralized the first one. Such was the law of the Medes and Persians.

Is *that* in the Bible?

Yes – in Esther 1:19; 3:1-15; 8:1-17 and Daniel 6:1-20.

Why was Daniel thrown into a lions' den?

Daniel found favor with all the kings under whom he served into his 90's. He distinguished himself because an excellent spirit was in him. The favor Daniel received provoked jealousy from governors and satraps (governors of Persian provinces), most especially because they could find no fault with him.

So they schemed to trap Daniel by persuading Darius the king to pass a law that for 30 days, no one could worship or pray to anyone except to Darius. Once that law was written, it became unchangeable – called the law of the Medes and Persians.

Darius was tricked into signing such a law. To his consternation, he found out that Daniel was turned in for breaking the king's law. Even the king couldn't change the law, his courtiers gleefully reminded him.

No amount of poring over the decree could yield a loophole for Darius and so the king reluctantly gave the command that Daniel be thrown in the lions' den. But he comforted Daniel and expressed confidence that Daniel's God would rescue him. The stone that was rolled over the lions' den was sealed with the same signet ring with which the king had sealed the decree that had been aimed at trapping Daniel.

Darius spent a fitful night, not sleeping or eating. In the early hours of the next morning, he rushed to the den of lions and started crying out for any response from Daniel. You can read the exciting conclusion to this story in Daniel chapter 6.

Is _that_ in the Bible?

Yes – in Daniel 6:1-20

To what pagan king did God reveal the history of the world?

Nebuchadnezzar.

He saw a great statue of awesome form. The head of gold represented Babylon, the chest and arms of silver represented Medo-Persia, the belly and thigh of bronze represented Greece, the legs of iron represented Rome, and the feet partly of iron and partly of clay represented the nations of Europe. The interpretation of this dream is based on a parallel history in a vision God gave Daniel in chapters 7 and 8 using the different imagery of beasts but providing the interpretation of the succeeding kingdoms of history.

Daniel not only interpreted the dream but he supplied the details because the king had forgotten his dream. God supplied both the details of the dream and their interpretation to Daniel. You can read this amazing story in the book of Daniel, chapter 2.

Is *that* in the Bible?

Yes – in Daniel 2.

How long was Manasseh's reign?

Even by modern standards, Manasseh reigned a long time – 55 years! Among modern monarchs, Emperor Hirohito of Japan reigned a span of 62 years and 2 weeks, Queen Elizabeth II of the United Kingdom was crowned in June of 1953 and King Bhumibol Adulyadej of Thailand, also known as Rama IX, ascended to the throne in June of 1946.

In Judah, King Manasseh reigned 55 years, a very long time by comparison with other kings of his era. The son of good King Hezekiah, Manasseh was a wicked king who did evil in the Lord's sight, rebuilding the high places which his father had destroyed, making his son pass through fire, practicing sorcery and using witchcraft.

Yet when he was led into exile to Babylon, he turned to the Lord, humbled himself greatly and God received his entreaty, heard his prayer and brought him back to Jerusalem. His was the longest evil reign, yet Manasseh found mercy when he turned to the Lord, because the Lord loves to show mercy.

Is *that* in the Bible?

Yes – in 2 Kings 21:1-2; 2 Chronicles 33:1-20.

How long can a person expect to live?

The Guinness Book of World Records lists the world's oldest living people each year and they usually are on this side of 120. Past record holders listed some on the other side of 120.

A longevity specialist has estimated 120 years as about what a person can expect to live to. With better lifestyle management and better nutrition, that age seems to be more and more reasonably attainable. Each year there are more centenarians added to the list.

That would square with what God said. Man used to live much longer – hundreds of years! - but because of his wickedness, he was restricted to something less. God decreed, "My Spirit will not put up with humans for such a long time, for they are only mortal flesh. In the future, their normal lifespan will be no more than 120 years."

Is _that_ in the Bible?

Yes – in Genesis 6:3.

Will all of God's plans come to pass?
Gener Paulo A. (Samboy) Quiambao

A loving God longs to restore all of fallen creation. He is not willing that any should perish but that ll people should come to repentance, and through that repentance avail themselves of God's provision for salvation.

However, because of their power of choice, many will choose their own way and reject salvation. A loving God will sorrowfully see many of His created beings fail to receive His free gift of salvation. And though it is His most fervent desire that whosoever believes in His Son Jesus should not perish but have everlasting life, it will not be the case for every living person. Only those who exercise their power to choose Jesus will be saved.

Is that in the Bible?

Yes – in John 3:16; 2 Peter 3:9

Who was the Angel of the Lord?

Angels are mentioned several times in both the Old and New Testaments. But in the Old Testament, a specific name is occasionally used and in some translations it is capitalized – the Angel of the Lord.

This name is used for Jesus before he came to earth as man. He appeared to Hagar, Abraham, Moses, Balaam, Gideon, and Samson's parents, and in each instance, he was referred to as the Angel of the Lord. And in each of these passages, you will also read that this Angel of the Lord is referred to later in the passages as "God" or "the Lord."

Is *that* in the Bible?

Yes – in Genesis 16:7-13; 22:11-16; Exodus 3:2-7, Numbers 22:22-38; Judges 6:12-16, 13:13-22.

Who has the longest name?

Mahershalalhashbaz.

Is _that_ in the Bible?

Yes – in Isaiah 8:1

Who were Jannes and Jambres?
Aldwin (Ace) Apostol

Paul mentions Jannes and Jambres in his letter to Timothy. He refers to their performance of magic imitating the miracles of Moses when he appeared before Pharaoh. But there is no mention of their names in the Old Testament, the only bible available to Paul.

However, available to him at the same time as he was schooled in Jewish literature and history were other Jewish sources, including the Targum, which was an Aramaic translation and interpretation of the Old Testament. The Targum mentions these two Egyptian magicians.

Paul's mention of these two names was in connection with his characterization of those who resist truth: men of depraved minds and a counterfeit faith. They would progress no further for everyone would recognize what fools they are.

Is _that_ in the Bible?

Yes – in 2 Timothy 3:8-9.

How is Jesus the Alpha and the Omega?

To the Jewish way of thinking, the most important positions are the first and the last, whether on a list, in a ranking or in any mention of multiple names.

Thus Jesus is the First and the Last, the Beginning and the End, and the Alpha (which is the first letter of the Greek alphabet) and the Omega (the last letter).

Is *that* in the Bible?

Yes – in Rev. 1:8; 21:6, and 22:13. (Though not specifically explained in the Bible, the Jewish understanding of first-and-last position importance can be verified separately.)

What was so unusual about a man carrying a pitcher?

Jesus sent His disciples to get a room ready for the observance of Passover. He told them how they would find the right place – by following a certain man who would be carrying a pitcher. This was intended as a sign. There would be very little chance of confusion or running into the possibility of finding another man carrying a pitcher of water because this act in itself was very unusual. In that culture, only women carried water in a pitcher.

Is *that* in the Bible?

Yes – in Luke 22:7-13

What was the Olivet Discourse?
Scott Leon

The Olivet Discourse is the name Bible scholars give to the extended teaching given by Jesus on the Mount of Olives a few weeks before His crucifixion. This was given in response to questions by the disciples after Jesus, noting the people's interest in the temple, said that the time was coming when not one stone would be left on top of another. The disciples wanted to know "when will these things be and what will be the sign that all these things will be fulfilled."

Jesus then referred to Daniel, defined the beginning of sorrows, described the abomination and the desolation following, and pointed out that a parallel event would happen in the time of the end. The destruction of the temple occurred in 70 AD when the Roman army led by Titus destroyed Jerusalem. The temple was burned and the gold melted and ran down the cracks between the stones. People realized this and later, in their search for the gold, took each stone apart from each other, thus fulfilling Jesus' prophecy.

Not all that Jesus prophesied was fulfilled in the destruction of Jerusalem. The rest will be fulfilled in a parallel event in the last days as another abomination of desolation will occur.

Is _that_ in the Bible?

Yes – in Matthew 24:1-25:46; Mark 13:1-37; Luke 21:5-36.

What is the Abomination of Desolation?

Edison Apostol

Jesus was warning His audience a few weeks before His crucifixion that Jerusalem would be destroyed before the generation He was addressing would pass. He also gave a clue to recognize when this event would happen. He said that when armies would surround Jerusalem and desecrate the holy place, then Jerusalem's desolation would soon follow.

This desolation happened in 70 AD when Jewish historian Josephus wrote that more than a million Jews were killed in one day by the Roman army. But not one Christian perished. They had remembered Jesus' words and fled to Pella, 15 miles from Galilee.

Enraged that the Roman army would desecrate their holy area, the Jews fought valiantly and beat the Roman army back. This was the signal to flee to anyone who remembered Jesus' words. Jesus even warned not to be caught in the city under those conditions on the Sabbath day. At sundown on Friday when the Jewish Sabbath began, the gates were closed to bar any merchant from doing any business within the city on the Jewish holy day. Not only would they be trapped in the event that the Roman army would attack on the Sabbath, but Jesus also said woe to nursing mothers and pregnant women. They would be handicapped in any escape attempts.

In fact, the 70 AD attack by Titus was not the first. It was the third but final and successful one. There were two previous attempts, in 66 by Roman Governor Felix and 68 by Vespasian before Nero committed suicide. The following year, Vespasian was confirmed emperor by the Roman Senate, leaving his son Titus to complete the invasion and eventual destruction of Jerusalem in 70.

Jesus intended that the Abomination that led to the Desolation of Jerusalem would also point to the last-day application when a similar abomination will trigger the desolation of the cities from which Christians awaiting their Lord's return would be urged to flee. That last-day event, Jesus said, would happen within one generation of the beginning of sorrows.

Is *that* in the Bible?

Yes – in Matthew 24:15, 19-20; Mark 13:14; Luke 21:20-21.

What is the Beginning of Sorrows?
Dipak Upreti

Jesus described conditions that would happen towards the end time. After he described them, he gave them a name – the beginning of sorrows.

What are these conditions?

They include wars, earthquakes, famines, pestilences, and celestial signs. When they collectively come together, then we know it has begun. And they will begin to crescendo and increase in frequency and intensity, like the labor pains a pregnant woman experiences. We live in a time when the frequency and intensity of natural disasters are hard to miss.

Is *that* in the Bible?

Yes – in Matthew 24:6-8, 29; Mark 13:7-8, 24-25; Luke 21:9-11, 25-26, 1 Thessalonians 5:3.

When will be the beginning of sorrows?
Donna Baluyot

Paul wrote to the Thessalonians about the day of the Lord and warned that people will not anticipate its coming. He said it would come as a thief in the night, indicating unexpectedness. Then he added that people would say "Peace and safety" but that this attitude of business as usual and confidence in their circumstances would be exactly when sudden destruction would come upon them.

He drew a metaphor of a pregnant woman in labor pains. As the birth event approaches, the pains come more frequently and intensely. So would it be with the last day events that make up the "beginning of sorrows." The wars, earthquakes, famines, pestilences and celestial signs would all be happening more frequently and with more intensity. This is exactly the situation in the world today.

Is _that_ in the Bible?

Yes – in 1 Thessalonians 5:1-3

What was the holy place that Jesus referred to?
Carmi Flores

It was not the first apartment of the wilderness sanctuary, which was also known as the Holy Place.

Jesus was describing the coming destruction of Jerusalem and gave a clue to when it would happen. He said that it would be when the holy place would be violated by an army. He referred back to an Old Testament prophecy and said that this would be what Daniel had referred to. The term used was "abomination."

What specifically was this abomination that people were to recognize? It would be whatever desecrated the holy place by violating its boundaries. In this instance, the holy place was an area of several furlongs beyond the perimeter of Jerusalem that would be included in the city's boundaries. (It would be similar to the sovereign area of any country that is surrounded by water. The boundary would not be the country's coastline but several miles extending into the ocean.)

Remember now that Jerusalem was known as the holy city. So the space surrounding the city was what Jesus referred to as the holy place. It was desecrated by the Roman army because at the head of the army was a standard on a pole on which was an image that bore the semblance of the emperor. This head was set under the wings of an eagle, another symbol of Rome. This standard was worshiped and sacrificed to before the army went to war.

Its symbolism was offensive to the Jews, who diligently obeyed God's commandment not to make any graven image or to worship it. They responded to this desecration of their holy place by fighting so fiercely in defense of their city that the Roman army was beaten back on each of three military campaigns (66, 68, and 70) before it finally broke through a second time in 70.

Is *that* in the Bible?

Yes – in Matthew 24: 15; Mark 13:14; Luke 21:20.

How did Jesus define Abomination?
Aanand Limbu

"Standing where it ought not."

Jesus referred the reader to Daniel, where Gabriel asked when the transgression of desolation would occur. But He also supplied the definition and described the events to follow.

The army would surround Jerusalem and be standing within the precinct considered by the Jews to be holy. Its very presence would constitute a desecration of the holy place because at the head of the army was the pole carrying the Roman standard, at the top of which was the image of a man, one that was worshiped before any military campaign. This graven image was considered an abomination by the Jews because of God's second commandment prohibition from making or worshiping graven images.

Jesus said that this abomination that causes desolation was spoken of by the prophet Daniel. Daniel had written "He will confirm a covenant with many for one week. In the middle of the week he shall bring an end to sacrifice and offering."

Is _that_ in the Bible?

Yes – in Exodus 20:4-6; Daniel 8:13, 16, 9:17; Mark 13:14, Luke 21:20.

Is using a picture of Jesus a violation of the second commandment?
Mahendra Thapa

The second commandment forbids making an image of anything in heaven above or on earth beneath or in the water under the earth. Taken in the most literal sense, this would forbid all art, including photography. This would be most impractical and does not line up with what God intended – He directed the Israelites to sculpt images of the two cherubim above the ark and to weave pictures of angels into the veil that separated the Holy Place from the Most Holy Place of the sanctuary.

Graphic designers and artists create images of what they think Jesus may have looked like as part of the communication process, enhancing the written account with graphic illustrations. But these are not intended or used for worship, which is part of the second commandment prohibition.

Is _that_ in the Bible?

Yes – in Exodus 20:4-6, 25:10-22, 36:35.

How were the people to respond to this Abomination?

Viroj Siriwattanakamol

They were to flee to the mountains.

There would be no looking back. No earthly possession could justify the risk of being killed in the ensuing desolation. In another era, demonstrating how accurate Jesus words were that where our treasure is, there our heart would be also, Lot's wife could not resist looking back. Disobeying the instructions of the angel who had urged them to flee, she was instantly turned into a pillar of salt.

Jesus warned the people that when they knew the Abomination had come, they were to flee to the mountains and depart from Judea because desolation would soon follow. Those in the country were not to even return to enter Jerusalem. This would be time for flight. To underscore the seriousness and severity of the event, Jesus said woe to pregnant and nursing women because of the hardship they would have to endure in fleeing. And He said they were to pray that the event would not overtake them in winter or on the Sabbath.

The gates would be closed on the Sabbath and anyone in would be killed if the invading army attacked on the Sabbath. Jewish historian Josephus wrote that over a million Jews perished in a single day. Those who remembered Jesus' words and acted on His warning were spared. His words were clear. The circumstances were well defined. Jesus told them to flee in order to escape the desolation which would surely follow.

The same kind of circumstances will happen in the last days as Jesus' warning had future end-time application.

Is *that* in the Bible?

Yes – in Genesis 19:24-26; Matthew 24:15-16, 19-20; Mark 13:14-19; Luke 21:20-21

What will be the last-day Abomination?
Viroj Siriwattanakamol

The abomination associated with the destruction of Jerusalem in 70 AD was that the flag pole carrying the standard and image of a man's head (the emperor's) was brought by the Roman army into the precinct surrounding Jerusalem which was also considered holy. The image of the man's head was under the wings of an eagle. The eagle was hated by the Jews because it was a symbol of evil, apostasy, anti-God, and suppression. Its metaphor was retained in Revelation in the fourth living creature. The eagle was also the standard of the northern tribe of Dan – a symbol of evil, apostasy, anti-God, and suppression. Thus the phrases "standing in the holy place" and "standing where it ought not" define abomination in Jesus' description of the coming destruction of Jerusalem.

What will be its counterpart in the last days? Well, it would have to fit the definition of "trampling" in the sense of the imposition of a requirement that would force people to violate their conscience with regard to worship. The word "transgression" in Daniel is *pasha* in Hebrew and means rebellion against the fourth commandment.

The trampling of Jerusalem by the Gentiles will be repeated in the end times when cherished Christian beliefs will be similarly trampled under by those who will impose national laws governing worship.

Is _that_ in the Bible?

Yes – in Daniel 8:13; Matthew 24:15; Mark 13:14; Luke 21:20, 24, Revelation 4:7.

Who is the Antichrist?
Charles Danuwar

The original anti-Christ was Satan fighting Jesus in heaven. Satan was defeated and fell as lightning from heaven. Satan now on earth tries to make everyone anti-Christ. The Bible says that he successfully finds key leaders in the continuing war against heaven.

Paul graphically talks about the Antichrist as a *man of sin, wicked*, and *son of perdition.* His is a contrarian behavior. He opposes everything and exalts himself above everything, including God. By exalting himself above God, he is being anti Christ. The term "sitteth in the temple" shows that he acts as if he is that Supreme Being. God calls all of this activity part of the "mystery of iniquity."

Characterizations of this hateful man all portray him as being a benefactor of everyone, a nice person, and a miracle worker, but underneath he is serving Satan. Note the progression of his activity as recorded in the three gospels. First he is "surrounding", then he is "standing in" (has entered) and now he is "standing in the holy place" (standing in the temple). He also defies and blasphemes God.

Every one of these descriptions reveals a power or organization which at the end of time will be deceptive and sinister with a cloak of "goodness" to turn people against Christ.

Is _that_ in the Bible?

Yes – in Matthew 24:15; Mark 13:14; Luke 10:18; 2 Thessalonians 2:3-8; 1 John 2:18, 22; 4:3; 2 John 1:7; Revelation 12:7

Why did Jesus tell the people to pray that their flight not be in winter or on the Sabbath?

Lota Apostol

The warning referred to a future event that was fulfilled in the siege of Jerusalem and temple destruction by the Roman army led by Titus in 70 AD. The practical advice was to flee the city before escape was not possible, such as on the Sabbath when the gates were closed starting at sundown Friday. Those who heeded the counsel fled to the small town of Pella, near Galilee and were spared. The Jewish historian Josephus witnessed the destruction of Jerusalem and reported that more than 1 million Jews perished in one day. Only those who heeded Jesus' warning escaped.

Is _that_ in the Bible?

Yes – in Matthew 24:16, 20. Mark 13:18;

When would barren and infertile women be blessed?
Eijie Abquilan

Jesus was referring to the coming destruction of Jerusalem when He said that those who would not be saddled with nursing babes would be blessed because they would be able to escape the coming desolation without the disadvantage that would accompany those who were pregnant or nursing.

A few weeks earlier, Jesus delivered the same warning regarding the coming destruction of Jerusalem (see Abomination of Desolation above) as He discoursed from the top of Mt. Olives. This time He was delivering the same message as he labored carrying the cross. He was responding to the sorrow of the women who followed, mourning and lamenting Him.

Is _that_ in the Bible?

Yes – in Luke 23:26-29

How many years are there in a generation?
Zernan Diaz

Forty.

This fact was established by the wandering of Israel in the wilderness as a result of their disobedience to God's command to take the Promised Land as their inheritance God had promised their ancestors. Sending 12 spies to scout the land, the people received wonderful reports of a land flowing with milk and honey but also of being populated by giants, by comparison to whom they seemed like grasshoppers.

The complaints displeased the Lord and He consigned the people to wander in the wilderness until all of that generation of adults 20 years and older would pass, with the exception of Caleb and Joshua. The number of years it took to complete this cycle was 40 and it became the measuring stick by which to define a generation. Jeremiah was called to preach one generation before Babylon fell. For forty years, he stood before the nation as a witness for truth and righteousness in a time of unparalleled apostasy. During the terrible sieges of Jerusalem, he was to be the mouthpiece of Jehovah.

Is _that_ in the Bible?

Yes – in Numbers 14:33-34; 32:13; Psalm 95:10; Jeremiah 7:29; Acts 13:18; Hebrews 3:15-17.

What did 40 mean in Bible times?
Zernan Diaz

Jesus fasted for 40 days. The floodwaters rose for 40 days. Elijah ran for 40 days.

Which figure is literal and which one is figurative?

To this day in the Middle East, the number 40 means an age of accountability, such as 18 is in the United States. To say "I'm 40" means "I'm old enough" even if that person may be only in his twenties. As part of the English language and in the American culture, one can say "I'm 18" to mean "I'm over 18," as in "I can do whatever I please, I'm 18." It means "I'm old enough to make my own decisions." A person usually says "I'm 18," even if he is over 18 to emphasize his attainment of independence.

In a similar way, the number 40 in the Bible can mean "large enough" or "a long time" and must be determined by context.

When Elijah ran from the fury of Jezebel who vowed to take his life the next day, he fled for 40 days and 40 nights to Horeb. This was most likely intended to mean "a long time" and not an exact number. Mt. Horeb from Judah would take less than 40 days to reach, especially if you're running for your life.

The 40 days and 40 nights of rain that caused the flood can be taken either literally or in the same manner to mean "a long time." Even the language describing the end of the flood says "it came about at the end of forty days...: (note the word "about"). However, subsequent numbering in the flood narrative seems to indicate that the number 40 is literal in this instance.

Moses went into the midst of the cloud into the mountain and was there 40 days and 40 nights. This would mean "a long time." The next time he went up, it was to obtain substitute tablets for those which he had broken in the matter of the golden calf, and that too took 40 days and 40 nights. This too would be "a long time" and not a literal figure.

But the spying out of the Promised Land took a literal 40 days, and the number of years Israel was consigned to wander in the wilderness was "according to the number of days which you spied out the land, forty days, for every day you shall bear your guilt a year, even forty years...." This was a literal 40.

So was the number of years that David reigned. And Solomon. The listing of the reigns of any monarchy would include exact numbers, not approximate ones.

The Bible contains many more references to the number 40. When you run across them, remember culture and custom. And remember context.

Is _that_ in the Bible?

Yes – in Genesis 7:12, 17; 8:6; Exodus 24:18; 34:28; Numbers 13:25, 14:33-34; Deuteronomy 2:7, 8:4; 1 Kings 2:11, 11:42, 19:2-8;

Who else besides Josephus corroborated biblical history?
Leizl Joy Briza

Some people think that part or all of the Bible is myth, fable or collection of fanciful stories not to be taken seriously. Such historical observations as those by Josephus would lend credence to Bible history. Josephus was a first-century Jewish historian and Roman citizen who wrote about the destruction of Jerusalem in 70 A.D. and a first century Jewish perspective of world history.

In addition to secular documents such as reports to Rome by Pilate, there is the internal evidence of names of contemporary people for whom there is additional secular documentation. The New Testament mentions people whose reigns, administrations, or existence can be verified historically – such as Caesar Augustus, Quirinius, the several Herods, Pilate, Felix, Claudius Lysias, Tertullus, Festus, and Agrippa.

The Old Testament similarly has numerous names whose mention helps fix exact or approximate dates for the books they are mentioned in – Nebuchadnezzar, Cyrus, Nabonidus, Nabopolasser, Darius, Artaxerxes, and Ahasuerus, among others.

Discoveries in archeology in the last two centuries have confirmed many remaining details that had no previous mention in secular history to confirm them.

Is *that* in the Bible?

Yes - All the names mentioned above are in the Bible and can be checked in any Bible concordance.

Did Bible writers quote from outside sources?
Marven Adap

Paul received information from others by word of mouth. He referred to reports of contentions that were declared to him by those of Chloe's household. He quoted from the printed word, as in the Cilician poet Aratus who had lived about 315-240 B.C. when he said "For we are also His offspring," crediting "as also some of your own poets have said." Paul was referring to God who made the world and everything in it when he said that in Him we live and move and have our being and that we are His offspring. The complete quote by Aratus was "It is with Zeus that every one of us in every way has to do, for we are also his offspring."

Paul also quotes from a third-century B.C. Athenian writer, Menander, to show that our lives are influenced by what we believe and with whom we associate (1 Cor. 15:33); and Epimenides, a well-known Cretan poet of the sixth century B.C. who was regarded as a prophet by his countrymen, to illustrate the poor reputation of the Cretans in the ancient world.

Is *that* in the Bible?

Yes – in Acts 17:24, 28; 1 Cor. 1:10-11, 15:33; Titus 1:12.

What is the glory of God?

Debora Munnu Rai

When Solomon dedicated the temple, the glory of God filled the temple so that no man could enter. The Hebrew word for *glory* indicates "weight" and "splendor" so the atmosphere in that temple must have been heavy. Also, bright. Ezekiel had a similar experience in seeing God's glory filling the temple.

The appearance of the glory of the Lord on Mt. Sinai was to the children of Israel like a consuming fire on the mountaintop. Their reaction was one of fear as they trembled at the thunderings and lightnings from the mountain.

When Joshua pleaded with Achan to confess his sin, it was not so that he could avoid punishment but so that in telling the truth he would be bringing glory to God. Although Achan confessed his sin, the judgment against him was not reversed. The objective of the confession was to glorify God. Bishop Patrick quotes the Samaritan chronicle, making Joshua to say here to Achan, *Lift up thy eyes to the king of heaven and earth, and acknowledge that nothing can be hidden from him who knoweth the greatest secrets.*

As Stephen was being martyred, he, being full of the Holy Spirit, gazed into heaven and saw the glory of God, and Jesus standing at the right hand of God.

God's name, character, and attributes are reflected in His glory. Moses had asked to see God's glory and as He passed before Moses, the Lord proclaimed, "The Lord, the Lord God, merciful and gracious, long-suffering, and abounding in goodness and truth, keeping mercy for thousands, forgiving iniquity and transgression and sin, by no means clearing the guilty, visiting the iniquity of the fathers upon the children and the children's children to the third and the fourth generation." The glory of God expresses the fullness of His character, including both justice and mercy. That character manifested itself in the words and ministry of Jesus.

The Bible speaks of light in the context of God's awesome presence by using the word *glory*. The New Jerusalem has no need of sun or moon in order that they might give it light, for the glory of God has illuminated it, and its lamp is the Lamb.

Isaiah and John the Revelator paint a picture of utter holiness in the glorious presence of God. The word "holy" and "glory" seem to go together for them. In the description of the glory that surrounds God's throne, there is a rainbow around the throne from which proceed lightnings, thunderings and voices.

Is *that* in the Bible?

Yes – in Exodus 19:16; 24:17, 33:19; 34:5-7; Joshua 7:19; 1 Kings 8:10-11; Isaiah 6:3; Ezekiel 44:4; John 17:1-5; Acts 7:55; Revelation 4:3, 5, 8, 21:23.

Who are the 144,000?
Letty Protacio

The number 144,000 is not a literal number. This would limit the number of people who will be saved. They are described as having written on their foreheads the name of the Father (who isn't willing that any should perish but that all should come to repentance). The number then symbolizes all faithful saints. They are described as virgins (those who have remained true to God and not prostituted themselves through false worship or idolatry), without fault (unblemished because they are in Christ) and singing a new song (their testimony, a song of redemption which only the redeemed – here identified as the 144,000 – can understand).

The math is easily followed in the listing of the 12 tribes times 12,000 sealed per tribe. Symbolically, the numbers reveal a greater depth – one of completeness. A thousand was the basic military division in the camp of Israel, the result of 10x10x10, a perfect cube symbolizing completeness. Multiply this thousand by 144 (12x12), symbolizing the faithful remnant from the Old and the New Israel (that is, the church – including believing Jews and Gentiles; all true believers in Christ are the Israel of God, Gal. 3:29 and 6:16) and you will get 144,000.

Is *that* in the Bible?

Yes – in Number 31:4-5; Galatians 3;29, 6;16; 2 Peter 3:9; Revelation 7:4-8; 14:1-5.

What is the Millenium?

Rendex Hart

The term indicates a thousand years.

The Devil is identified as being bound during this period, denoting that he will be prevented by circumstances of the desolate planet from deceiving the nations.

Those who had suffered for their witness to Jesus and for the word of God will reign with Christ during this millennium. It is to them that judgment of the wicked dead will be committed. This judgment is described in legal terms: the books were opened, and the wicked dead would be judged according to their works as recorded in the books.

After the millennium, the wicked dead are raised, Satan is released to deceive the nations, and he will gather all of them together to battle.

Is _that_ in the Bible?

Yes – in Revelation 20.

Why will God wipe away all tears?
Letty Banaag

During the millennium, the righteous will sit in judgment of the wicked dead. That will be the time when will be answered all the questions about why certain loved ones did not make it to heaven. That will be an agonizing moment for all who sit in judgment of their loved ones, and tears of regret, sorrow and sadness will flow.

But following the millennium, the New Jerusalem will descend from heaven to earth and God will wipe away all tears after that period of judging the wicked dead. There will be no more death, nor sorrow, nor crying, for the former things have passed away. God said He will make all things new. There will no longer be reason for tears. They will have been wiped away.

Is _that_ in the Bible?

Yes – in Revelation 21.

What is "mystery"?
Marie Aleli C. Haboc

The term "mystery" means something formerly hidden but now revealed. It also cannot be understood except by divine revelation. The secret thoughts, plans and dispensation of God remain hidden from unregenerate mankind, but are revealed to all believers. This is what Jesus explained to His disciples when they asked Him, "Why do you speak in parables?"

His answer quoted Isaiah: "Seeing they may see and not perceive, and hearing they may hear and not understand."

This mystery which has been hidden for ages and from generations, has now been revealed to His saints: Christ's sinless life, atoning death, powerful resurrection, and dynamic ascension.

Is *that* in the Bible?

Yes – in Isaiah 6:9-10; Mark 4:11; Colossians 1:26.

What was the purpose of Jesus' parables?
Ernie Banaag

The purpose of parables was to make a spiritual truth clearer to hearers. The form of parables also made it easier to remember the truths communicated. If there were any in the audience who would otherwise be hostile, they would not take offense in the point of the parable since they could not receive the truth or would be unable to discern it.

The disciples asked Jesus why He taught the people in parables and He replied that it was because the mysteries of the kingdom had not been given for their understanding. It had been given to His disciples to know the mysteries.

Is *that* in the Bible?

Yes – in Matthew 13:10-14; Mark 4:10-12; Luke 8:9

What was the point of the parable of the Talents?

Sam Young

Stewardship, investment and risk-taking in God's service.

A man traveling to a far country called his servants to distribute assignments to them: different amounts of investment capital for their portfolios, five talents to one, two talents to the second, and one talent to the third. This was not an arbitrary allocation but one based on their management ability.

Upon his return, the first two stewards presented a doubling of their investment trust. The third, though, had buried the investment capital entrusted to him and dug it back up to return it. The master was pleased with the first two servants but not with the third. He said that the least he could have done was to deposit it at the bank to accrue interest.

So he ordered the investment capital taken from the third servant and given to the first.

Jesus intended to illustrate the requirement for developing opportunities for greater service by correctly deploying the gifts and abilities entrusted to our care. Neglecting to do this would not only cause one to miss out on new opportunities but also lose out on that which was entrusted to us.

Jesus said that whoever has, to him more will be given, and he will have abundance – a reference to wise investment. He contrasted that with him who does not have, even what he has will be taken away from him.

Is *that* in the Bible?

Yes – in Matthew 13:12, 25:14-30

Why does God give some people power to get wealth?

John Farrior

God directed Israel to let any Hebrew slave go free who had served his years of indenture. But in sending such away, he was to supply him liberally from his flock, from his threshing floor and for his winepress. He was to give from what the Lord had blessed him with. God gives blessings to be shared, not hoarded.

And in order to establish His covenant which He swore to Israel's ancestors, God reminded Israel that it was He who gave them power to get wealth. God's covenant was to bring Israel into the Promised Land. He knew that prosperity often brings arrogance, causing us to forget that God is the source of all blessing. Therefore the command was that they should remember that it is the Lord God who gives the power to get wealth.

This power to get wealth is a gift from God.

Is *that* in the Bible?

Yes – in Deuteronomy 8:18; 15:14; Ecclesiastes 5:19

Is Jesus delaying His coming?

John Jena

Peter warns that in the last days scoffers will come, mocking the truth and following their desires. They will say "What happened to the promise that Jesus is coming again?"

But the Lord isn't really being slow about His promise, as some people think. It is for our sakes that He is being patient because He doesn't want anyone to be destroyed, but wants everyone to repent. What appears to many to be a delay is in reality the Lord's unwillingness that anyone should perish.

The Lord patience gives people time to be saved.

Is _that_ in the Bible?

Yes – in 2 Peter 3:3-4, 8-13, 15.

What should be the response of those awaiting Jesus' return?
Migy T. Reswand

While they are waiting for these things [Jesus' coming unexpectedly like a thief, accompanied by the heavens passing away with a terrible noise and the very elements disappearing in fire], they are to make every effort to be found living peaceful lives that are pure and blameless in His sight. They are to live holy and godly lives.

They are to be on their guard so that they will not be carried away by the errors of wicked people and lose their own secure footing. And they are to grow in the grace and knowledge of our Lord and Savior Jesus Christ.

Is _that_ in the Bible?

Yes – in 2 Peter 3:11, 14, 17-18

How is Jesus our Advocate?
Divinia P. Wilkinson

John's epistle to the churches surrounding Ephesus where he spent his retirement years was written to encourage the members that they may not sin. However, if they sinned, John sought to assure them of help by drawing an analogy to a court in the legal system. In this analogy, the sinner is the accused.

The Advocate would be our Lord Jesus Christ who pleads our case before the Father. An advocate is a defender, a lawyer. Because His sacrifice on Calvary atones for all sins, Jesus has the right to plead His sacrifice on our behalf. He is our Advocate.

Is _that_ in the Bible?

Yes – in 1 John 2:1-2

Why are we to pray for laborers?
Zeny B. Mupas

Jesus sent out 12 disciples, (and in another instance 70 disciples) to go to the lost house of Israel. He sent them out two by two into every city and place where He Himself was about to go to. As part of His instructions, He impressed on His disciples the urgency of the work they were about to embark on and the need to pray. The need to pray was a result of His heart being moved with compassion.

As He went about all the cities and villages, teaching, preaching, and healing, Jesus was moved with compassion for the people because they were weary and scattered like sheep having no shepherd.

They were to pray the Lord of the harvest for laborers to bring in the harvest. The sowing had been done and it was now time for the reaping. He expressed it thus "The harvest truly is plentiful but the laborers are few."

Is _that_ in the Bible?

Yes – in Matthew 9:37-38; Luke 10:1-2

Why were the disciples not to greet anyone along the road?

Migurawanala Ven Disauranjok

Then (as today in third world countries), greetings between acquaintances who met along the road tended to be drawn out (even farewells today are done in stages – in the living room, at the door, in the parking lot, etc.).

Jesus was underscoring the urgency of the mission on which He was sending His disciples. Nothing could deter them from their task, especially not the courtesies accompanying greetings and salutations.

Time was of the essence and could not be wasted. People would be receiving the opportunity to respond to the gospel and any rejection of the message would be final (their lot would be worse than that of Sodom and Gomorrah).

Thus the need to conserve time and to manage it well.

Is _that_ in the Bible?

Yes – in Luke 10:4

Why did God ordain marriage?
Lou Vincent May

God said that it wasn't good for man to be alone and so He created Eve for Adam. Marriage was one of two institutions established in the Garden of Eden (the other was the Sabbath). In the ensuing centuries and millennia, God used this institution to portray His relationship with His chosen people and all who would enter into a relationship with Him.

Thus He borrows from the marriage relationship to say that He hates divorce, He asks for single-minded faithfulness, He detests split loyalty and likens it to prostitution, and He invites intimate communion, creating rich imagery for His desired relationship with us. He draws all of that from terms in the marriage relationship. The judgments against Israel for their idolatry, which is compared to prostitution, was also couched in marriage language: they would have no birth, no pregnancy, and no conception; and they would have a miscarrying womb and dry breasts (the result of not obeying God). Yet God offers "to betroth you to Me forever."

The language of today's marriage vows reflect some of these concepts in scripture: "forsaking all others" ("no other gods before Me"; "cannot serve two masters"); "for better or for worse" ("The Lord will not fail you or forsake you"); "in sickness and in health ("Father of mercies who comforts us in all our afflictions"), "in prosperity and adversity" ("I am the Lord, I do not change"; "see, I have set before you today life and prosperity") and "till death do us part" ("He who promised is faithful").

Even in pointing to Jesus' return, analogy is drawn from preparations for marriage. The parable of the ten virgins builds on this as understood in their cultural context. Jesus' promise to go away "to prepare a place" refers to the Jewish custom of having the groom build a room addition to his father's house before returning to collect his bride. The wedding banquet is yet another picture.

We understand God's love in marriage terms we can relate to and we understand Jesus' return in the analogy to wedding preparations.

Is *that* in the Bible?

Yes – in Genesis 2:18-22; Exodus 20:3; Deuteronomy 30:15, 31:8; Hosea 2:19; 3:3, 4:10-13; 9:1, 11, 14; Malachi 2:16, 3:6; Matthew 22:2-12, 25:1-13; John 14:1-3, 2 Corinthians 1:3-4; Hebrews 10:23.

What is a tentmaker?
Glory N. Ersola

Paul supported his ministry by repairing tents. When he went to Corinth, he found a Jew there by the name of Aquila who with his wife Priscilla moved there when Claudius commanded all Jews to leave Rome. Because Paul and Aquila were of the same trade, they worked together as tentmakers.

Except for the Levites, there were no full-time "gospel workers" as we might call them today. Each one who was called to the Lord's work supported himself with a trade. Borrowing from Paul's experience, we today say that a self-supporting missionary is a "tentmaker."

Is *that* in the Bible?

Yes – in Acts 18:3

What is a minor prophet?

Preyapone Pumturn

The term is not used in the bible but is our designation for the authors of the last 12 books of the Old Testament whose names the books bore. Perhaps the most well-known minor prophet would be Jonah. Each of the minor prophets had a message of warning for their time, many of them with end-time application.

The messages were not minor in any sense of the word except for length, when compared to other prophetic books. So "minor" indicates only brevity, not substance or importance.

Is _that_ in the Bible?

Yes –See the last 12 books of the Old Testament.

Who was Amos?

Amos Sinchuri

We'll use Amos, a minor prophet, as a representative of minor prophets in order to profile them. In addition to their calling, these minor prophets had their "tentmaking" activities. Amos' principal activity was as a shepherd who tended sycamore-fig trees. The minor prophets all had messages of warning. Amos' message was one of judgment on Israel and on seven neighboring nations of Israel.

Amos' message was that true religion demands righteous living. Two of the better-known quotes from his book are: "Can two walk together unless they are agreed?" and "Surely the Lord God does nothing, unless He reveals His secret to His servants the prophets."

Is _that_ in the Bible?

Yes – in Amos 1:1, 3:3, 7.

Why will the plowman overtake the reaper?
Jade Manez

Along with the messages of warning that Amos preached came a message of hope. It promised restoration to the nation of Israel, a repair of its damages and a rebuilding on its ruins. The captives of Israel would be brought back and inhabit what was formerly wasted cities. They would plant lush vineyards and eat the fruit from their gardens. It is a wonderful picture of restoration that ends with the promise that they would be reestablished in their land so that they would no longer be uprooted from the inheritance that God had given them.

In describing the abundance of this restored land, Amos said that the plowman would overtake the reaper and the treader of grapes him who sows seed. So bountiful would the yield be that when it came time to plant again for the next season, they would still be harvesting from the previous season.

Is _that_ in the Bible?

Yes – in Amos 9:11-15

Why did Zacchaeus climb the sycamore tree?

Zacchaeus was a chief tax collector. He was among the crowd who eagerly wanted to see Jesus as he passed through Jericho. Although Zacchaeus must have stretched his neck and stood on his toes, he couldn't see over the shoulders of the people who lined the road because he was short of stature.

Running ahead, he picked a tree to climb to gain a vantage point. It was a sycamore tree, related to the fig tree but hardier and taller. Now he would be able to see Jesus.

This was also an evangelistic moment for Jesus.

He looked up the tree and immediately sized up the situation. Although Zacchaeus was there because of his short stature, he would also be avoiding people because he was a tax collector. Tax collectors were notorious for their usurious and dishonest practices and they were universally despised.

But Jesus invited Himself to Zacchaeus' home, an act considered to be one of honor in that culture. The people groused about this. What happened during that visit? Read the joyful conclusion of this story in Luke 19.

Is _that_ in the Bible?

Yes – in Luke 19:1-9.

Why were the wise men "late" in arriving to celebrate Jesus birth?

The wise men were students of the stars who had observed a heavenly phenomenon (a star in the East) which they interpreted as a sign of the birth of the King of the Jews. So they traveled from their home in Persia to Jerusalem in search of the babe, sleeping by day and traveling by night, the better to follow the bright star that led them.

Their query "Where is He who has been born King of the Jews?" so unsettled King Herod that he vowed to eliminate this pretender to the throne. He inquired of the chief priests and scribes where Christ was to be born and they quoted the prophecy that identified Bethlehem. Next he had to determine how old the child was, and to do this he asked the wise men how long it had been since they had first seen the star.

Finally he had to find out where this babe was, so Herod persuaded the wise men to bring him a report so that he too could "worship" the new king. The star that had guided them into Jerusalem but disappeared from the night sky now reappeared to lead the wise men and stood over where the young child was. Notice that Jesus was no longer a babe but a child, and neither was he any longer in a manger. The Bible narrative says that the wise men came into the house where the child and his mother were. Jesus' parents had moved into a house from the animal stall where Jesus had been born.

This new address was what Herod eagerly desired from the wise men's reports he had prevailed upon them to give him. But God warned the wise men in a dream not to return to Herod and so they returned to their country another way.

Traveling from a far-off country took over a year and so the wise men in our timeline appear to be late as our understanding goes. They don't seem to historically and accurately belong in a crèche or nativity tableau. But no one is really ever late to come to Jesus. So the wise men rejoiced greatly to have been able to see the child Jesus and they went home rejoicing. Their interpretation of the stars, very likely a divine gift with some insight from a prophet named Balaam, had led them on a joyous journey to worship.

Is _that_ in the Bible?

Yes – in Numbers 24:17; Micah 5:2; and Matthew 2:1-12.

What were the gifts for a king?

The wise men came from the East to welcome the king they had understood to be the king of the Jews when they saw his star in the east. As befitting a king, they brought with them gifts of gold, frankincense and myrrh.

When the angel later instructed Joseph to take his family immediately to Egypt and stay there until summoned, they had these precious gifts to fall back on by converting them into currency for their subsistence.

These gifts were most appropriate also for their symbolism: gold for kingliness, frankincense for the priestly role, and myrrh, a bitter herb, for the suffering he would endure and the sweet fragrance of his sacrifice. Myrrh, an ingredient in perfume and the holy anointing oil, was used in embalming. It had a bitter taste and was added to wine to desensitize from pain anyone condemned to death. This drugged wine was what Jesus was offered at the cross.

Is _that_ in the Bible?

Yes – in Exodus 30:23; Esther 2:12; Psalm 45:8; Proverbs 7:17; Matthew 2:11, 13-14, 19-21; Mark 15:36; 27:48; John 19:28-29, 39.

What is a sackbut?

Bojo Lijauco

It is a music instrument. Many old names have modern equivalents, and music instruments also developed, and their names changed. In this case, the sackbut was an ancient trombone.

Other music instruments we would recognize by their modern names include the dulcimer – which looked somewhat like a guitar and was plucked, not strummed; and the psaltery – a multi-stringed zither, plucked with a plectrum (like a guitar pick).

Is *that* in the Bible?

Yes – some mention of old instruments occurs in Daniel 3:5, 7. The KJV uses the old terms.

Why did Jesus curse a certain fig tree?

It would seem rather uncharacteristic of Jesus to curse an unfruitful tree, most especially when the narrative says that it wasn't the season for figs.

But there was an explanation known to Jesus' listeners but unknown to us. Had his audience not had this agricultural insight, they would have mentioned the unreasonableness of Jesus' expectation of fruitfulness, just as today's reader might. But no such response is recorded.

A fig tree's leaves in the spring promise a fruitful yield because they are accompanied by the appearance of knobs on the branches. These knobs are not only harbingers of a future yield but can also be eaten for food. They have a pleasant taste and would have provided Jesus the nourishment he sought to satisfy his hunger. The knobs eventually drop off but six weeks after their first appearance, the fig fruit appears.

That the healthy foliage wasn't accompanied by knobs meant that the tree would not be fruitful at all later. It would not produce what it was intended by its existence. Therefore it was as good for nothing now as it would prove later to be. As a fig tree, it had failed its mission in life. It would take only a few more weeks for that conclusion to be fully demonstrated, but its future was most evident right now to the local observer. Jesus cursed the fig tree's barrenness and lack of production.

The lesson to be learned is about the expectation of productive fruitfulness in appointed responsibility and service.

Is _that_ in the Bible?

Yes – in Mark 11:12-14, 20-21

Why did Nicodemus seek Jesus out by night?

The day would come when members of the Sanhedrin Nicodemus and Joseph of Arimathea would step forward and ask Pilate for the body of Jesus to give it a proper burial. They would also start to use their support and influence more openly for the fledgling church after the resurrection.

But in the early going, they stayed under the radar. Nicodemus, an influential member of the Sanhedrin didn't want it known that he was sympathetic to Jesus and his following. In order to not jeopardize his position in the Sanhedrin where he would be more valuable to the cause, he sought Jesus out by night.

He had questions and wanted answers, and he quickly established his acknowledgment of Jesus as a teacher come from God, because "no one can do these signs...unless God is with him." Jesus wasted little time in throwing Nicodemus a curve, saying "unless one is born again, he cannot see the kingdom of God."

"How," Nicodemus asked, perplexed, "can one enter again into his mother's womb and be born?"

You can read Jesus' answer and the rest of their interesting dialogue, including the context of the most well-known passage in scripture – John 3:16 – by reading the first 21 verses of the third chapter of the gospel of John.

Is _that_ in the Bible?

Yes – in John 3:1-21; 19:38-40.

Why did Joseph try to put Mary away privately?

The Bible attributes Joseph's unwillingness to expose Mary to the shameful procedure of repudiating her publicly before witnesses as allowed by custom, to his being a just man. Instead, he decided to put her away privately.

What was behind all this?

Mary was engaged to Joseph. In the custom of the day, a betrothal, or engagement, was as binding as a marriage and could be broken only by divorce. But Mary had become pregnant and the penalty for adultery could be as severe as stoning. While thinking about protecting her reputation by putting her away privately, Joseph received an angelic visitation in a dream. The angel told Joseph not to hesitate to take Mary as wife, explaining that her conception was by the Holy Spirit.

Is _that_ in the Bible?

Yes – in Matthew 1:18-21. (In Deuteronomy 22:23-24, the words *engaged* or *betrothed* and *wife* are used to refer to the same woman.)

When did a certain bridegroom not recognize half his bridesmaids?

In one of Jesus' parables. It was about a bridegroom and ten bridesmaids.

The bridesmaids of the day were called *virgins* and they formed part of the welcoming group awaiting the appearance of the bridegroom. The bridesmaids would then accompany the bridegroom to the wedding banquet, which was considered the wedding ceremony. But the bridegroom's appearance was not known in advance, only that it would be soon.

A lesson was being drawn about the appearance someday of Jesus who is portrayed as a Bridegroom and who will return to receive His bride, which is the church, and the need for our constant readiness.

When a man and woman became engaged, they were considered as good as married. In anticipation of starting their married life together, the man would go away to his father's house to build a room addition to receive his bride. This absence could take up to a year but when he was ready, he would return to take his bride to his father's house. This joyous occasion was marked by a wedding banquet. The bridesmaids were among those waiting to celebrate the occasion.

This custom was the metaphor for one of Jesus' promises. He said he would go to prepare a place for us in His Father's house which contains many rooms and then return to receive us to Himself. (In some translations the word *mansion* is used for *room.*)

Among the ten bridesmaids waiting for the bridegroom, five of them were called wise (because they had come ready with lamps full of oil) and five of them were called foolish because they had made no similar provision. While waiting for the bridegroom to appear, everyone had fallen asleep.

When the cry went out that the bridegroom was arriving, everyone jumped up and trimmed her lamp. Unfortunately, the foolish virgins or bridesmaids didn't have enough oil and so they begged the wise bridesmaids to share some of their oil. Their response was that they didn't have enough but they counseled the five foolish bridesmaids to go to those who sold to buy some oil for themselves.

They did, but when they returned, the bridegroom had come and those who were ready went with him to the wedding banquet and the door was shut. The five foolish bridesmaids knocked on the door but the answer was that the groom didn't know who the bridesmaids were. (This puzzling reply is more fully explained in a following entry.)

The parable is one about preparedness for Christ's second coming.

Is *that* in the Bible?

Yes – in Matthew 25:1-13; John 14:1-3.

What does it mean to trim one's lamp?
Gregg S. L. Ovalime

All the virgins waiting for the bridegroom trimmed their lamps. What did that mean?

The Greek word for "trim" is *kosmeo,* the basis for the word *cosmetic.* To trim is to beautify, arrange, decorate, furnish, embellish, adorn, put in order. That's what a bride and her bridesmaids do in preparation for a wedding.

The use of the word *trim* pictures a period of revival before the Second Coming of Christ. Today is the time to trim our lamps in anticipation of the greatest event in history to which we look forward.

Is *that* in the Bible?

Yes – in Matthew 25:7

How are people to prepare for Jesus' return?
Grayce Sarmiento

The point of many of Jesus' parables, like that of the ten virgins, is one of preparedness for His return. We are to watch and be sober, putting on the breastplate of faith and love and as a helmet the hope of salvation.

Jesus warned that we should take heed, lest our hearts be weighed down with carousing, drunkenness, and cares of this life. We are to watch and pray always that we may be counted worthy to escape all these things that will come to pass, and to stand before the Son of Man.

Take heed. Watch. And pray.

Is *that* in the Bible?

Yes – in Mark 13:33-37; Luke 21:34, 36; 1 Thessalonians 5:6, 8

What will be some earmarks of Jesus' second coming?

Peter L. Giespy

It will not be in secret. Every eye will see Him. There will be no isolated appearances such as in the desert or only to a few. But false prophets will appear and deceive many saying "I am he" and "The time has drawn near." We are not to go after them.

His coming will be unexpected, like a thief in the night.

There will be a false sense of peace and security, of business as usual. When people say "Peace and safety!" then sudden destruction shall come upon them, as labor pains upon a pregnant woman (with increasing frequency and intensity).

This condition that is accompanied by increasing frequency and intensity is known as the beginning of sorrows and is seen in the signs of wars, earthquakes, famines, pestilences and celestial signs.

Jesus will descend from heaven with a shout, with the voice of the archangel and with the trumpet of God. It will be a glorious event that no one alive can miss.

He will come in the glory of the Father and of His angels.

The dead in Christ will rise first.

Is *that* in the Bible?

Yes – in Isaiah 25:9; Daniel 12:2; Matthew 16:27; 24:11, 31, 26:64; Mark 13:6, 22; Luke 9:26; 21:8, 23:30; 1 Thessalonians 4:16; 5:2; Revelation 1:7.

Who will be resurrected to meet Christ?

Rebekah Shrestha

Just as the same sun that melts wax will harden mud, the glorious event of Christ's return will produce different responses. The wicked will say to the mountains, "Fall on us!" and to the hills, "Cover us!" but the redeemed will say, "Behold, this is our God, we have waited for Him, and He will save us."

There are two types of individuals who will rise at this special resurrection at Christ's return: 1) the righteous dead; and, 2) those who are raised to shame and everlasting contempt. Who are these who are raised to everlasting contempt? This prophecy by Daniel is unfolded by Revelation (Daniel is unsealed in Revelation). There it says that every eye will see him coming in the clouds including those that pierced Him.

Those that mocked the Son of God and doubted His divine origin and commission will witness for themselves the glorious return of Him whom they mocked, whipped, scourged and crucified. Jesus answered the high priest who put Him under oath to declare if He was the Christ, the Son of God, by saying "You have said it. And in the future you will see the Son of Man seated in the place of power at God's right hand and coming on the clouds of heaven."

Is _that_ in the Bible?

Yes – in Isaiah 25:9; Daniel 12:2; Matthew 26:64; Luke 23:30; Revelation 1:7.

What does it mean to "know"?

It must have been a strange response from the bride-groom to those who were shut out of the wedding banquet and were desperately knocking at the door to be let in. He said "I don't know you."

The Greek word translated "to know" is at the root of the word *knowledge*. Its idea is that it has a beginning and a continuing progress to an attainment.

That very nicely sums up the kind of relationship we are to have with Jesus. The underlying idea of *know* is the perception of truth by personal experience. We need to experience the Lord and we are encouraged to have moments of quiet in order to enter into that experience. We are to be still and experience God as God.

Jesus sought to emphasize this by portraying Himself as standing at our heart's door knocking and seeking entrance. If allowed in, He would enter into an intimate relationship with us described by the sharing of a meal. It is an unhurried getting to knowing each other. This can be our experience each morning in our time of devotions and meditating on God's word and prayer. In that sharing of the meal, we can be reminded that Jesus is the Bread of life.

It is by knowing Jesus (*experiencing* Jesus) that we are saved, not by knowing about Jesus. Jesus sought to impress this point even more by describing those who try to earn the right to get to heaven by doing good things. He said they will plead their case by asking "Lord, have we not prophesied in Your name? Have we not cast out demons in Your name? Have we not done many wonders in Your name?" These are the people who depend on works and effort to earn salvation.

Jesus said that He would have this word for them, "I never knew you; depart from Me." He will mean, "We never had the time to experience each other. I am the Way, the Truth, and the Life, but you never developed a relationship with Me."

This intimate relationship He desires with us is demonstrated in the use of the word "know" for marital relations. Adam *knew* his wife and she conceived and bore a son. Similarly, our experience of intimacy with the Lord will birth new life in us and through us.

In Jesus' prayer before the Garden of Gethsemane experience, he defined eternal life as coming to *know* the only true God and Jesus Christ whom He had sent. And we are invited to be still and experience God. Experiencing God involves having regular quiet times and expectant waiting before Him.

Is *that* in the Bible?

Yes – in Genesis 4:1, Psalm 46:10; John 6:48; 8:32; 14:6; 17:3; Matthew 7:21-23; Revelation 3:20. The Greek word for "to know" is *ginosko*.

Why did a certain homebuilder build on sand?

Sand is not a very good foundation for building a house. Rock would be better and is expected to be the kind of foundation that homes are built on. So why did this homeowner build his house on sand?

This was a parable and Jesus sought to differentiate the two responses to His teachings. He drew a comparison between them. Those who heard His teachings and did them were wise and were likened to a man who built his house on a foundation of rock. This is excellent foundation and will render his house in good stead in the event of rain, floods and stormy gales.

But those who heard His sayings but didn't do them were likened to a man who built his house on sand. This was very foolhardy because sand isn't very solid foundation. And when the rain, floods and winds came, the house fell flat.

Is *that* in the Bible?

Yes – in Matthew 7:24-27

How did Paul address his letters?
Dirarsen Lovas

A characteristic of letters written in Paul's time was to start with the sender's name, not end with it as we do today. After announcing that he is the writer and including a brief portrait of who he is, there follows a brief salutation containing a blessing, then a listing of the addressees, before the writer goes into the substance of his message.

So Paul would start by saying "Paul, a bondservant of Jesus Christ, called to be an apostle, separated to the gospel of God" (Romans); "Paul, called to be an apostle of Jesus Christ through the will of God" (Corinthians); "Paul, an apostle (not from men nor through man, but through Jesus Christ and God the Father who raised Him from the dead)" (Galatians); "Paul, an apostle of Jesus Christ by the will of God" (Ephesians); "Paul and Timothy, bondservants of Jesus Christ" (Philippians); "Paul, an apostle of Jesus Christ by the will of God, and Timothy our brother" (Colossians); "Paul, an apostle of Jesus Christ, by the commandment of God our Savior and the Lord Jesus Christ, our hope" (1 Timothy); "Paul, a prisoner of Christ Jesus, and Timothy our brother" (Philemon).

And addressed "to all who are in Rome, beloved of God, called to be saints" (Romans); "to the church of God which is at Corinth (1 Corinthians); "to the churches of Galatia" (Galatians); "to the saints who are in Ephesus and faithful in Christ Jesus" (Ephesians); "to all the saints in Christ Jesus who are in Philippi, with the bishops and deacons" (Philippians); "to the saints and faithful brethren in Christ who are in Colosse" (Colossians); "to the church of the Thessalonians" (1 Thessalonians); "to Timothy, a true son in the faith" (1 Timothy); "to Titus, a true son in our common faith" (Titus); "to Philemon our beloved friend and fellow laborer, to the beloved Apphia, Archippus our fellow soldier, and to the church in your house" (Philemon).

With a blessing in the salutation: "Grace to you and peace from God our Father and the Lord Jesus Christ" (Romans, 1 Corinthians, Galatians, Ephesians, Philippians, Colossians, Thessalonians, Philemon); "Grace, mercy, and peace from God the Father and the Lord Jesus Christ our Savior" (Titus). If you look up these references, you'll find an extended blessing following each of these salutations.

Is *that* in the Bible?

Yes – in the opening verses of Romans, 1 & 2 Corinthians, Galatians, Ephesians, Philippians, Colossians, 1 & 2 Thessalonians, 1 & 2 Timothy, Titus and Philemon.

Why should we not cast pearls before swine?

Would you cast expensive pearls before swine? No one would think of doing that then or today. So it was a good basis on which Jesus could build a case for discernment.

Swine don't eat pearls. They don't know the value of pearls so they can't appreciate them for their true value. If you feed swine pearls, they may be looking for something to eat and, determining pearls not to be food, turn against you and attack you in angry response. In the process of doing all that, they may also be trampling those same pearls under-foot. What a pity!

So if swine don't value pearls, there is no sense in giving them pearls. That is precisely the point that Jesus wanted to make. A little discernment and a dose of good judgment are necessary when communicating the gospel. Not only is it counterproductive for you to insist on giving the good news to those who resist it but it can boomerang against you.

Is _that_ in the Bible?

Yes – in Matthew 7:6.

What is Corban?
John Bayalkoti

Jesus decried how the Jews put tradition and man-made rites above the spirit of the law. He said "All too well you reject the commandment of God, that you may keep your tradition." He pointed out that they had set aside the fifth commandment in order to be able to carry out the tradition of the elders.

That tradition dictated that they could by saying "Corban" designate a piece of property to be donated to God by setting it aside to benefit the temple. But in so doing, they not only deprived their parents the support that the property could give them, but the donor also could enjoy the free use of the property during his lifetime.

Saying "Corban" allowed a person to dishonor and defraud his parents in life and after death, under the guise of a pretended devotion to God. In this way, Jesus said they dishonored God by ignoring the spirit of the fifth command-ment, saying that they made "the word of God of no effect" through their tradition.

Is _that_ in the Bible?

Yes – in Mark 7:5-13.

How many servants were involved in the parable of the talents?

In the Matthew parable, we would naturally assume three, because to one servant the man who was about to depart into a far country gave five talents, to a second servant he gave two talents, and to another he gave one talent. Talent in this instance isn't natural ability but a measure of weight. It was worth about $1000. However, its application can include natural ability and gifts and servants can wisely employ opportunities given to them. The first two servants wisely invested what was entrusted to them, but the third one didn't.

In the Luke account (not a parallel because of significant differences in the parables), the nobleman called ten servants to whom to distribute minas. A mina was approximately 50 shekels. There is a parallel in the number of servants who gave account of their investments (three).

These two parables were given when Jesus was approaching Jerusalem and because he was eager to correct the people's understanding of the advent of the kingdom of God. They thought it was imminent. Jesus sought to underscore not only its delay but their responsibility in making optimum use of opportunities to increase the kingdom. They were to "Do business till I come."

Part way through the Luke account (verse 14) is a reference to a historical event. Luke says that the nobleman's citizens hated him, and sent a delegation after him, saying, "We will not have this man to reign over us." The Jewish historian Josephus wrote that after the death of Herod the Great, the

Jews sent a delegation to Rome to protest the appointment of Herod's son Archelaus who had gone to Rome (v. 12) to be confirmed as king of Judea.

Is *that* in the Bible?

Yes – in Matthew 25:14-30; Luke 19:12-26.

Why did Ezekiel lie down on his right side for 40 days?

In order to dramatize his messages, God instructed Ezekiel to act out some of these messages. These acts prophetically pictured what would happen to the people or the city.

In one of those messages, God told Ezekiel to bear the iniquity of the house of Judah by lying on his right side for forty days. Each day would represent an actual year of punishment that Judah was suffering.

God assured Ezekiel that he would not be able to move from that position until the days of bearing the iniquity of Judah would be completed. In this position, he was to prophesy against Judah. If this seems like a long, long time to be stuck in one position, consider that Ezekiel's forty days followed over one year (390 days) of lying on his left side to bear the iniquity of the house of Israel.

These acted-out messages drove the point home quite dramatically. Some of them were judgment, many of them contained hope. There were several more such acted-out messages – from eating a scroll, saving the shaved hair from his head and beard to weigh and divide (to bind some in his garment and throw the rest into the fire), digging through a wall, going into captivity, prophesying his wife's death on the day of her death, to walking into a river one thousand cubits at a time by actual measurement. Each of these prophetic acts was followed by a word or a prophecy that Ezekiel spoke. The acted-out message was reinforced by a spoken message to explain what he portrayed.

Sometimes the people would ask him the meaning of what he was acting out. No doubt the strange way of communicating his message got the attention of the people. The word God used for him was "sign." Ezekiel would be a sign to the house of Israel.

Ezekiel also saw many visions from which he received his messages to deliver, many times being lifted up by the Spirit to transfer him from one place to another. Very often, his messages began with "Moreover the word of the Lord came to me, saying...."

Is _that_ in the Bible?

Yes – in Ezekiel 4:1-7; 8:7-8; 12:1-6; 24:15-19; 35:1; 36:16; 47:1-8

What was Ezekiel's bread?

Many brands of Ezekiel bread are sold today in health food stores, trading on the mystique of Ezekiel's bread. Ezekiel's bread was special because God gave him the recipe.

While he was lying on his left side for 390 days, he was to sustain himself with bread made from wheat, barley, beans, lentils, millet, and spelt – about eight ounces a day (20 shekels by weight). Not only was the bread weighed but so was his water measured so that he would drink about two-thirds of a quart (one sixth of a hin) daily.

These acts would be a sign that the people would eat bread by weight with anxiety and drink water by measure with dread, because of Israel's iniquity.

Is _that_ in the Bible?

Yes – in Ezekiel 4:9-17

What did God specify should accompany worship?

Grayce Sarmiento

Offerings.

God directed the Israelites to observe the Feast of Unleavened Bread, admonishing them further not to appear before Him empty. It wasn't only at this feast but at each of the three feasts each year to which God summoned His people that He directed them to bring the first of the first-fruits of the land into the house of the Lord as an offering. None should appear before Him empty-handed.

The connection between any act of worship and the presentation of an offering is further reinforced by the Psalmist who wrote *Give to the Lord the glory due His name; bring an offering and come before Him. Oh, worship the Lord in the beauty of holiness!*

Is _that_ in the Bible?

Yes – in Exodus 23:14-19; 34:18-26, 1 Chronicles 16:29; Psalm 96:8

Why are offerings important?
Mark DiMaggio

It is more blessed to give than to receive. And the act of giving is to be associated with worship. God directed Israel not to worship Him empty-handed. One of the reasons that Satan deprived Job of all his possessions was to prevent him from being able to worship. When finally he was able to worship because God directed his friends to provide the sacrifice to allow Job to intercede for them, Job's fortunes were reversed. It started with his ability to give a sacrificial offering as part of worship.

The blessing of giving was something God was eager for His people to learn. Their history shows that they responded magnificently as in the bringing of their gold and silver articles and jewelry to be melted down and used in the construction of the tabernacle. Moses had to say "Stop, we have enough already; indeed, too much."

Jesus said that when we give, it shall be given back to us in the same manner as we give. But nothing is ever returned only in the same measure. It always returns in greater measure. A seed sown and grown will bring a larger harvest than was planted.

When we tithe, we cause the enemy (the "devourer") to be paralyzed ("rebuked") for our sakes so that he won't be able to touch our families ("vine in the field") or our finances ("fruit of your ground"). Instead, our tithing will open the sluice gates ("windows") of heaven. Water from a dam when flooding from heavy rains or snow runoff can rise to dangerous levels. When released through the sluice gates. it pours out in a torrent, not a trickle. Thus we are assured that we won't have enough room to contain the blessings that result from tithing, which was intended for the support of God's work ("meat in My house").

Is _that_ in the Bible?

Yes – in Exodus 23:15, 34:20, 36:6-7; Job 42:8, 10; Malachi 3:10-11; Luke 6:38; Acts 20:35

When did an army of dead bones come to life?

Ezekiel again was in the middle of this. The Lord sent him on another acted-out message and the first step was for him to prophesy to a whole valley of dead bones. So he commanded the bones to have sinews and flesh come into them and covered with skin. He prophesied them to live and with a rattling the bones came together, bone connecting to bone.

Now though they had muscles and skin, the bones still had no life. So Ezekiel prophesied breath to come into them from the four winds and that's exactly what happened. The bones then came to their feet, an exceedingly great army.

What was the acted-out message?

The bones were the whole house of Israel. They indeed said "Our homes are dry, our hope is lost, and we ourselves are cut off." But by God's word through Ezekiel, they were restored. The wind of the Spirit was promised to sweep through Israel bringing the miracle of new life.

The song "Dem Bones" celebrates this event.

Is _that_ in the Bible?

Yes – in Ezekiel 37:1-14

Why did it take 21 days for an angel to reach Daniel?

Angels are messengers sent by God on specific assignments. (The word *angel* is translated from a Greek word meaning *messenger.*) The image of angels' travel is one of speed, in one instance flying in the midst of heaven. However, one particular angel went on assignment and it took him 21 days to reach his destination. He was sent to Daniel in response to his prayer and search for meaning to the visions he had received. However, he was delayed by the prince of the kingdom of Persia. This is a picture of spiritual warfare with a hierarchy of spiritual powers. The angel was finally assisted by a more powerful angel by the name of Michael. After he finished assisting Daniel in understanding his visions, the angel took his leave and said he still needed to fight another principality – the prince of Greece – on his return.

Is _that_ in the Bible?

Yes – in Psalm 103:20; Daniel 10:13 and 20; Heb. 1: 14; Revelation 14:6

What is the usual posture of an angel?

The redeemed sit at the right hand of honor in heavenly places. That's because they are seated there in Christ Jesus, whose position is at God's right hand. But angels don't have that privilege. In scripture, whenever angels are mentioned, if they aren't bowing in worship, their posture is always one of standing.

Michael is described as the great prince who stands watch over the sons of your people. When Gabriel was sent to speak to Zacharias to foretell the birth of John the Baptist to his barren wife Elizabeth, he said "I am Gabriel who stands in the presence of God, and was sent to speak to you and bring you these glad tidings."

Is _that_ in the Bible?

Yes – in Daniel 12:1; Luke 1:11, 19; Ephesians 1:20, 2:6

Are we allowed to eat snakes?
Jeiel Abquilan

God's original diet for Adam and Eve in the Garden of Eden included every seed-bearing plant and fruit from trees. After the flood, there was no vegetation from which to derive food and so God gave Noah permission to eat of every moving thing. Along with that permission came the first food restriction, and that was that the flesh should not be eaten with its blood.

In time, God codified for the children of Israel which flesh foods would be acceptable and those that would not be. A list of examples was given but it could by no means be comprehensive. And so God provided some specific parameters by which to judge what flesh foods could be eaten.

Animals which both split the hooves and chewed the cud were to be acceptable. The camel could not be on that approved list because it did not have split hooves, though it chewed the cud. Neither the pig, who has split hooves but does not chew the cud.

Among marine life, fish that had both fins and scales would go on the approved list, whether fresh- or salt-water fish. Among the birds, those that were scavengers were to be avoided. Winged insects that walked on the ground would not be acceptable for food unless they also had jointed legs so that they could jump. This would include locusts, crickets and grasshoppers.

Any animal that walked on all fours and had paws would be unclean. Small animals that scurry along the ground or slither along their bellies would be unclean. This would include the snake.

The Lord gave as the reason for strict observance of these dietary laws the need for His people to consecrate themselves and be holy "because I the Lord your God am holy." Eating the unclean foods would defile the people, He said. Modern science has validated the dangers of eating foods in the "unclean" list. To enjoy optimum health today, a diet that conforms to the guidelines given here or, better yet, to the original diet given to Adam and Eve, would promote better health and avoid disease.

Is *that* in the Bible?

Yes – in Genesis 1:29; 9:3-4; Leviticus 11.

What was Paul's affliction?
Neph Manez

Paul suffered from a physical affliction that isn't specifically identified (many scholars believe it had to do with his eyesight). This affliction he called a thorn in the flesh (an intense, wearying challenge or affliction) and further defined it as being a messenger from Satan.

Paul pleaded with the Lord three times that this affliction might depart from him, but God assured him that His grace would be sufficient for Paul to endure the affliction. Lest he should boast in his exalted position by the abundance of revelations given him, Paul accepted this affliction to keep him humble and dependent on God's strength. He emphasized the basis of his strength: "When I am weak, then I am strong."

God's Grace is always sufficient.

Is _that_ in the Bible?

Yes – in 2 Corinthians 12:7-10

When can people fast and still eat?

Intercessors fast for a variety of reasons. For those whose physical constitutions may not permit a full fast, they go into a Daniel fast. What is a Daniel fast?

Daniel fasted for 21 days for understanding and interpretation of the vision that had been given him, the length of time that paralleled the time it took the angel to reach him to give him interpretation. But he must have eaten sparingly because he lists those things that he avoided – desserts, meat and wine. So the Daniel fast is a very light fast.

Is _that_ in the Bible?

Yes – in Daniel 10:3

How did God's Son become a baby?
Glory S. Nytogaard

This is a wonderful story of the second member of the Godhead coming to earth and being born as a baby, living a sinless life, and dying on the cross to pay for man's sins. This portrays the depth of God's love for His children, for whom provision for their redemption was made before they were even created!

It involved a plan for God to live as a man to be exposed to the same temptations as we are and yet live a sinless life in order to be our Substitute to receive the penalty of death for sin - our sins. In order for Him to do that, He had to come down and be born as a baby. How this was accomplished is a mystery to us, one which we will never comprehend. We can only gratefully respond to it.

Is _that_ in the Bible?

Yes – in Matthew 2, Luke 3, John 3:16-17; Hebrews 4:15.

Why did God's Son have to die?

The majesty of Jesus' sacrifice on the cross towers over all history and all creation because through God's Sacrifice on Calvary, He sealed our pardon, insured our salvation, and defined his unfathomable love to the whole universe.

The penalty for sin is death, and we would have had to pay that penalty but for Jesus who paid it for us. He who did not deserve to die died so that we who did not deserve to live might live. Sin would have brought eternal separation for us from God, but Jesus' death bridged that chasm so that we are closer to God than if we had never sinned.

O wondrous love that God should die to save us from sin!

Is _that_ in the Bible?

Yes – in John 3:16; Romans 5:12, 6:23; James 1:15; 2 Peter 3:9. God's love is written on every page of the Bible.

Did Jesus ascend to Paradise on the day He was crucified?
HSD

Original manuscripts of the Bible did not have punctuations. They were written in all capital letters as lower-case letters were not developed until later. Punctuation, too, was not added until later.

The case of the misplaced comma finds its greatest challenge in Jesus' statement on the cross on Friday when He assured the thief, "Assuredly, I say to you, today you will be with Me in Paradise."

When Mary Magdalene was weeping at the tomb site two days later, Jesus appeared to her and told her "I have not yet ascended to My Father...." That compels us to reevaluate Jesus' statement to the thief. If He could not assure the thief of being in Paradise with Him that day, perhaps it was the fact that He spoke that applied to "today."

That would be the case if we move the comma to after "today." Jesus' statement now reads, "Assuredly, I say to you today, 'You will be with Me in Paradise.'" What this statement with the revised punctuation communicates is assurance to the thief of eternal salvation, not a promise of translation to Paradise that day.

The two separate statements by Jesus now harmonize.

Is _that_ in the Bible?

Yes – in Luke 23:43; John 20:17

What are the seven churches?
Vincent Manez

The apostle John recorded God's messages to seven churches, all of which existed in the cities mentioned. These churches had certain characteristics that were representative of churches of all generations. These letters as applied through history gave indication of how they stood spiritually before the Lord. Each letter exhorted the individual to become an overcomer.

These messages through the apostle had a pattern: 1. a commission to the messenger of the church named; 2. a character description of Christ; 3. a commendation (with the exceptions of Sardis and Laodicea); 4. a censure (with the exceptions of Smyrna and Philadelphia); 5. a correction; 6. a challenge; 7. a covenant promise as a gift to every member of the Body of Christ.

These historical churches were Ephesus, Smyrna, Pergamos, Thyatira, Sardis, Philadelphia, and Laodicea.

Is _that_ in the Bible?

Yes – in Revelation 2-3.

Why were tears collected in a bottle?
Rendex Hart.

The custom was for mourners to collect their tears in a small tear bottle. Some museums display these tear bottles from Jesus' time and earlier. These bottles were then buried with the dead.

The Psalmist was acknowledging God's faithful interest in his life to the extent of numbering his wanderings or recording everything about his life in a book. His metaphor? The tear bottle: God would collect the Psalmist's tears to put in His bottle. In so doing, God was noting the Psalmist's sacrifice, tears and everything else.

Is *that* in the Bible?

Yes – in Psalm 56:8

How many donkeys did Jesus ride on?

Jesus sent two of his disciples to bring a donkey and its colt to him in preparation for his triumphal entry into Jerusalem. That he would ride on a colt never before sat on would be consistent with many other symbols from the Old Testament that applied to Jesus.

And so artists portray Jesus as riding on a colt with its mother walking next to it. That would be implied from the Luke version of the story. But in Matthew, Jesus is described as sitting on both the donkey and the colt at the same time. Both animals had clothes thrown over them by the disciples for Jesus' riding comfort.

It would have been very impractical to have anyone ride on two animals at the same time, and perhaps that wasn't what happened. But that's the way it was mentioned in Matthew.

Is *that* in the Bible?

Yes – in Matthew 21:7; Luke 19:29-35

Did stones ever cry out?

As Jesus rode into Jerusalem, the people (referred to here as "disciples", the many others besides the apostles who were followers of Jesus) lined the streets and praised God with a loud voice for all the mighty works that they had seen in Jesus' ministry. They rejoiced, saying

> *Hosanna to the Son of David!*
> *Blessed is the King who comes in the name of the*
>   *Lord!*
> *Hosanna in the highest! (Peace in heaven and glory*
>   *in the highest!)*

This display didn't settle well in the spirit of some of the Pharisees and they admonished Jesus to rebuke the people. Jesus answered "I tell you that if these should keep silent, the stones would immediately cry out."

The stones didn't cry out that day but they would have, according to Jesus, had the Pharisees prevented praise from ascending from the people's lips.

Is _that_ in the Bible?

Yes – in Matthew 21:8-11; Luke 19:37-40.

When did a donkey speak in a human language?

Balaam was a reluctant and disobedient prophet who wanted to have the promised rewards from a pagan king while yet struggling to be faithful to his prophetic calling.

What Balaam was being hired to do was to curse God's people. Balaam correctly said that he couldn't do that. But instead of walking away from temptation, he continued to keep it alive by telling the king's messengers to stay overnight so that he could have opportunity to seek the Lord's word.

God spoke to Balaam in a dream, giving him permission to go with the men but to say only the word that God would speak to Balaam. But God was displeased with Balaam's response to the situation where he had strung out entertaining the proposal instead of walking away from it. So the Lord met Balaam on the way.

The donkey saw the Lord (read the separate entry regarding the Angel of the Lord) and turned aside to the field to avoid the Angel who held a sword in his hand. Balaam struck the donkey to make him return to the road. The Lord then stood in a narrow path between walls in a vineyard. The frightened donkey pushed herself against the wall to avoid the Angel, crushing Balaam's foot against the wall. In anger, Balaam struck the donkey again.

The Angel then went further and stood in a narrow place where there would be no way to turn one way or the other. Upon seeing the Angel, the donkey sat down and refused to budge. Enraged a third time, Balaam struck his donkey with his staff.

The Lord then opened the donkey's mouth and she said to Balaam, "What have I done to you, that you have struck me these three times?"

What an interesting exchange!

An animal spoke in human language. But instead of being taken back by this unusual phenomenon, Balaam did something that made him look the fool. Having been blinded by rage, he did something unexpected. He answered the donkey!

What did he say? You can read how this interesting exchange continued and how it ended, in Numbers 22.

Is *that* in the Bible?

Yes – in Numbers 22
Note: In spite of Balaam's disappointing behavior, he uttered some of the most beautiful Messianic prophecies – in poetic format – when he followed God's directions, Numbers 23. Then he became a statistic in the battle between Israel and the Midianites. Numbers 31:8.

What color is the Red Sea?

The Red Sea is not red.
There are seasonal red blooms of a plant near the water's surface. And the mineral-rich mountains nearby are red. In fact, where they appear is in Biblical Edom, which means "ruddy complexion." (Edom is the nation of the descendants of Esau, who was "red-faced.") It might have been because the sea bordered the Egyptian desert, which the ancient Egyptians called "the red land."
No one knows for sure why the Sea which the Israelites crossed to escape the Egyptian army was named the Red Sea. However, it is a fact that when the Old Testament was translated from the original Hebrew into the *koine* Greek of the New Testament (the result being the Septuagint), what was translated as Red Sea came from the Hebrew Sea of Reeds or Reed Sea.

Is *that* in the Bible?

Yes – references to the Red Sea include Exodus 10:19; 13:18; 15:4; 22; 23:31; Numbers 14:25; 21:4; 33:10-11,

Deuteronomy 2:1; 22:4; Joshua 4:23, 24:6; Judges 11:16; 1 Kings 9:26; Nehemiah 9:9; Psalm 106:7, 9, 22; 136:13, 15; Jeremiah 29:21; Acts 7:36 and Hebrews 11:29. "Reed Sea" is translated from the Hebrew *Yam suph.*

Why did God not lead Israel through the shortest route to the Promised Land?

Alma Lou Fordek

When Pharaoh finally let the Israelites go, God did not lead them along the main road that runs through Philistine territory, even though that was the shortest route to the Promised Land. He said "If the people are faced with a battle, they might change their minds and return to Egypt."

It was to keep them from getting dismayed by their circumstances or enemies that God mercifully led Israel in a roundabout way through the wilderness toward the Red Sea.

Is _that_ in the Bible?

Yes – in Exodus 13:17-18.

How did God open a path through the Red Sea?

John Puen

With a strong east wind.

In a demonstration of God's power, the children of Israel crossed the Jordan River into the Promised Land under miraculous circumstances when the river parted as soon as the priests (carrying on their shoulders the ark of God) stepped into the water.

Thus we tend to assume that 40 years earlier when their forefathers left Egypt, they crossed the Red Sea under similar circumstances. But there was a big difference. When Moses stretched out his hand over the Red Sea, the Lord caused the sea to go back by a strong east wind all that night that made the sea into dry land. Now the children of Israel were able to go into the midst of the sea on dry ground with walls of water on each side! It must have been an awesome sight.

It was the greatest miracle Israel experienced that was celebrated in song and the Psalms, ranking number one by its frequent mention in praise for God's awesome power.

Is _that_ in the Bible?

Yes – in Exodus 14:21-22; 15:1-21; Psalm 136:13-15.

How did Elijah go to heaven?

Many people answer this question with "in a chariot of fire". It was indeed a chariot of fire that appeared while Elijah and his servant Elisha were walking and talking, but it was not a chariot of fire that caught him up into heaven.

Elijah went up in a whirlwind.

It was in another incident during Elisha's ministry that chariots of fire were involved. There appearedon the mountain, when Elisha prayed that God would open the eyes of his servant, a lot of horses and chariots of fire all around them – evidence to back up Elisha's assurance to his servant earlier that those who were with them were more than the enemy.

Is _that_ in the Bible?

Yes – in 2 Kings 2:11; 6:16-17

What are "graduated numbers"?
Gideon N. Urarte

Hebrew poetry is quite different from western poetry where rhyme and meter are evident. Hebrew poetry depends more on parallelism or contrast of thought or idea. It also abounds in what we would call puns, playing on words for their similarity of sounds which nevertheless still communicated the intended irony or hidden meanings.

Among the more interesting literary features of Hebrew poetry is a device called graduated numbers. A certain number is stated and then exceeded by one more. Here are some examples: "For three transgression...and for four," in Amos, and in Proverbs: "Six things the Lord hates, yes, seven are an abomination to Him..." "There are three things that are never satisfied, four never say 'enough'" "There are three things which are too wonderful for me, yes, four which I do not understand..." "For three things the earth is perturbed, yes, for four it cannot bear up..." and "There are three things which are majestic in pace, yes, four which are stately in walk...."

Is _that_ in the Bible?

Yes – in Proverbs 6:16, 30:15, 18, 21, 29; Amos 1:3, 6, 9.

What were the three obligations of a man toward a slave wife?

If a man takes a slave wife and then subsequently takes another wife, the first wife has continuing rights to food, clothing and sexual intimacy, even as she continues being a slave.

If she is denied these, then she is set free from her slavery.

Is *that* in the Bible?

Yes – in Exodus 21:10-11

What does it mean to eat Jesus' flesh and drink His blood?
Gard R. Wymalife

Jesus had just declared Himself to be the Bread of Life. In response to this, the Jews quarreled among themselves asking, "How can this Man give us His flesh to eat?"

That's when Jesus said that unless they ate the flesh of the Son of Man and drank His blood, they would have no life in them. The Jews weren't the only ones puzzled by this statement. Jesus' perplexed disciples concluded "This is a hard saying; who can understand it?"

To eat the flesh and drink the blood of Christ is to receive Him as a personal Savior, believing that He forgives our sins, and that we are complete in Him. What food is to the body, Christ must be to the soul. Food cannot benefit us unless we eat it, unless it becomes a part of our being. So Christ is of no value to us if we do not know Him as a personal Savior. A theoretical knowledge will do us no good. We must feed upon Him and receive Him into the heart so that His life becomes our life. His Love, His Grace, must be assimilated.

Is *that* in the Bible?

Yes – in John 6:48-60

How much must a thief who is caught pay back?

Seven times more than he stole, even if he has to sell everything in his house. He is not despised if he steals to satisfy his hunger when he is starving, but if he is caught, then he must restore sevenfold.

Is *that* in the Bible?

Yes – in Proverbs 6:30-31.

Is honey good for you?
Bodem D. Koh

Only if eaten in moderation. Proverbs says "It is not good to eat much honey."

Equal parts honey and vinegar diluted in warm water make an excellent morning tonic. The Promised Land was described as flowing with milk and honey, an expression to denote abundance and goodness.

Honey is the only substance in which infection cannot set in because of the heavy concentration of sugar. Honey discovered in Egyptian pyramids thousands of years old still was acceptable food. Because of its concentration of sugar, honey can be used in an emergency as a salve on open wounds to prevent infection.

Is _that_ in the Bible?

Yes – in Exodus 13:5, 20-24; Deuteronomy 6:3; Proverbs 25:27

What did Mizpah mean?

Jacob had secretly stolen away from his father-in-law Laban with his whole household and possessions while Laban was away shearing his sheep. He had worked for Laban for 20 years and God had blessed Jacob so that, while he had arrived in Padan Aram 20 years earlier with nothing, he was leaving 20 years later a wealthy man.

But Laban had not treated Jacob right and had changed wages on him several times. Furthermore, Laban's sons grumbled about Jacob's wealth being made at their expense. So Jacob talked it over with his wives, Laban's daughters Leah and Rachel, and they agreed with the decision to leave.

When Laban was told on the third day that Jacob had left, he organized a posse and overtook Jacob seven days later in the mountains of Gilead. But God had warned Laban in a dream to speak neither good nor bad to Jacob.

After berating Jacob for leaving without so much as a thank-you or at least an opportunity for Laban to kiss and say goodbye to his grandchildren, Laban proposed a covenant. Jacob took a stone and set it up as a pillar and his household added to it so that the stones made a heap. In the custom of the day, Laban and Jacob established the covenant with a meal at that spot.

Then Laban declared the heap to be a witness to the covenant they were about to make and called it Mizpah, because he said "May the Lord watch between you and me when we are absent one from another."

The words sound very nice and we use them today as a parting blessing. But they were originally intended more as a warning and a threat. That point where they stood was their demarcation line and neither party was to wander into or invade the other party's territory. That's what they intended by the spoken words. So they called on the Lord to watch over both of them to make sure that they kept their covenant while away from each other and unable to enforce the non-aggression pact in person.

Another translation makes it clearer: May the LORD watch between us to make sure that we keep this treaty when we are out of each other's sight.

Is *that* in the Bible?

Yes – in Genesis 31:1-55.

How much did a bunch of grapes weigh?

Most of the biblical weights and measures are unfamiliar to us. There is the gerah, which is approximately 1/50 of an ounce or six-tenths of a gram, the beka which is 10 gerahs, or 1/5 of an ounce or 5.5 grams, and the pim which is two-thirds of a shekel, or 1/3 of an ounce or 9.5 grams. Of greater familiarity to us are the shekel which is two bekas or 2/5 of an ounce or 11.5 grams, and the mina which is 50 shekels, or 11/4 pounds or six-tenths of a kilogram.

The most familiar weight to us would be the talent, which is 60 minas or 75 pounds or 34 kilograms. The context within which we recall the talent is in Jesus' parable of a landowner giving his stewards varying amounts of talents to reinvest. We usually think of talent as a measure for gold or other precious metal. The talent was a measure of weight.

Our table grapes today would weigh about a mina, more or less. But the grapes in Canaan, the land God promised to his people, weighed considerably more than a talent. Yes, possibly more than the 75 pounds that a talent weighs. The land that was described as flowing with milk and honey produced bumper crops and the 12 spies brought back evidence as Moses had directed.

The spies had been sent to scout the land and its inhabitants and to bring back a report. The grapes they brought back were so heavy that they had to be carried by two men, with the grapes hanging from a pole between the men's shoulders.

And that was just one bunch!

Is _that_ in the Bible?

Yes – in Numbers 13:17-27

What is the Gideon multiplication?
Tom Hamilton

Lest anyone think that it was by any less than His power and grace that Israel triumphed, God sometimes chose the "least" from the tribes to step into leadership. He chose Saul whose only apparent redeeming features to the people were his handsomeness and height. But God could read his heart and found a humility that He could use.

When Samuel told Saul that he had been chosen, Saul replied, "But I'm only from the tribe of Benjamin, the smallest tribe in Israel, and my family is the least important of all the families of that tribe!" Thus God chose one for the highest office – king – from the least important family in the smallest tribe.

Before Saul and the monarchy, God ruled over Israel through judges. One of them was Gideon. When God gave him his marching orders, Gideon protested and said, "But Lord, how can I rescue Israel? My clan is the weakest in the whole tribe of Manasseh and I am the least in my entire family!"

Gideon finally agreed to accept his commission after much persuasion and after he asked for a sign through the use of a fleece. He asked that a fleece of wool on the threshing floor become wet with dew while everything around it remained dry. It was done. But he asked again, this time for the ground surrounding the fleece to be wet and for the fleece to remain dry. Again it was done.

So Gideon was convinced and called the men he had mustered earlier. But God told him that they were too many, lest Israel claim glory for itself in victory. So God directed Gideon to send home those who were timid or afraid and 22,000 left, leaving "only" 10,000 who were willing to fight.

But again the Lord told Gideon, "There still are too many!" So He devised a test to determine who would constitute the army and the Lord directed Gideon to bring his men down to the spring. They were told to drink from the spring as God had said that the manner in which they drank would determine Gideon's army.

Those who knelt down and drank with their mouths to the stream were eliminated, 9,700 of them. Only 300 made it to the army. What did they do to earn this privilege?

They remained battle ready and alert for the enemy.

At least that's how it looked when they dipped into the water and with their cupped hands to their mouths they lapped the water with their tongues like dogs.

How did they fare in battle?

Wonderfully! If you want to know the exciting conclusion to this strange army recruitment, you can read it in Judges 7.

The progressive "multiplication" of Gideon's army went in the opposite direction. So a Gideon multiplication is one that decreases, not increases.

Is *that* in the Bible?

Yes – in 1Samuel 9:1-2, 20-21; Judges 6:14-15, 7:1-7.

Why did the rich young ruler go away sorrowful?

There is a contrast between two rich men – one who was nameless but was held in high esteem in his community, and the other one who was held in contempt as all tax collectors were, but who had a name – Zacchaeus. Both sought eternal life but one went away sorrowful and the other received Jesus joyfully. Zacchaeus had turned from a life of extortion to give half of his goods to the poor and return fourfold anything he had taken from anyone by false accusation. To him Jesus said "Today salvation has come to this house."

But when He gave the rich young ruler the prescription in response to his question "What shall I do to inherit eternal life?" He counseled him to sell all that he had and distribute to the poor. The rich young ruler became very sorrowful, for he was very rich.

Is *that* in the Bible?

Yes – in Luke 18:18-23 and 19:1-9

In what way did Jesus identify the rich young ruler's need?

Jesus demonstrated an uncommon ability to gently convict people without embarrassing them. For the sake of a certain adulterous woman, Jesus wrote on the ground. To Simon the Pharisee, he told a parable. No one hearing the parable thought that it fingered Simon. Simon gratefully grasped the application privately.

So when a rich young ruler came to Jesus to ask what he should do to inherit eternal life, Jesus sized him up and read his heart. He knew that the young man had kept the law to his best ability but that also he was held by his riches.

Jesus responded to his question "What shall I do to inherit eternal life?" by starting to list the last six commandments – which the Jews recognized as encompassing their duty to their fellowmen. But Jesus left out one commandment, the tenth.

This omission enabled the rich young ruler to truthfully state "All these things I have kept from my youth." This was Jesus' diplomacy. Avoiding embarrassing his questioner and granting him the privilege of affirming his keeping of the commandments, Jesus then allowed the rich young ruler to confront his own weakness. He told the rich young ruler that he lacked one thing, but this could be remedied by selling all that he had and distributing the proceeds to the poor. Then he would have treasure in heaven and could follow Jesus as His disciple.

For the rich young ruler, this was the sticking point. Here was where the rubber met the road for him. He was rich and his attention was preoccupied by material wealth. There was nothing wrong in being rich, Jesus taught in other parables, as He had enjoined his audience to practice faithful stewardship for the sake of kingdom advance. But apparently in the rich young ruler's case, acquiring wealth was his goal, not distribution of wealth entrusted to us, which is our privilege in stewardship. In this, he would meet his test. God had given him the ability to acquire wealth and now it was the rich young ruler's opportunity to acknowledge that God is the Giver of all good gifts and that what is entrusted to us is for His glory and for kingdom advance.

The record says "he became very sorrowful, for he was very rich."

Is _that_ in the Bible?

Yes – in Matthew 19:16-22, Mark 10:17-22; Luke 7:36-50; 18:18-23; John 8:6.

If Jesus were to respond to a similar query from us today, He might not leave out that same commandment, but He might leave out the one that has to do with that by which we fall short of the kingdom. Jesus cares not only about our eternal salvation but also about how truth is brought to our attention, because He cares about our feelings. And He cares that we not have anything prevent us from inheriting eternal life.

How can we be perfect as God is perfect?

The passage that enjoins us to be perfect doesn't say for us to be as perfect as God is but that we should be perfect, just as He also is perfect. Even then, it remains a stumbling block to our understanding if we don't define the word *perfect*.

The original word which is translated *perfect* means *complete*. That is, to be complete at each stage of one's development.

Thus a tomato seed is perfect as a seed and when planted in good soil, will sprout into a seedling. At that stage it can be considered perfect in its development though it yields no tomatoes. A few weeks later, the seedling grows into a large plant with many green leaves. It looks perfect and is complete at that stage of its development, but there still are no tomatoes to harvest. Then buds appear and blossom into tiny yellow flowers. At that stage it is perfect – complete – in its development to that point.

The flowers drop off, the tomatoes form and grow large, but they're still green and unripe. Nevertheless, the plant is perfect in that it is complete in its development to that point. Then the fruit turns red and ripe and luscious. Even though the leaves start to wither and brown, this stage of development is perfect as we can consider it complete.

This progression of different levels of completion in our Christian life is what it means to be perfect – to mature at each stage and keep growing and maturing in Christian Grace. It is in that manner that one can be perfect.

Is _that_ in the Bible?

Yes – the text is in Matthew 5:48; the explanation would require an understanding of the original Greek.

Where is Mt. Moriah?

There was no more severe test given to man than that given to Abraham to offer his son Isaac as a sacrifice. This must have been puzzling to Abraham who had been promised a son through whom God would fulfill his covenant, but Abraham obediently surrendered to God's command. You can feel the tension in the narrative and the wonderful provision God made for the resolution of this test by reading the whole account in Genesis 22.

The mount on which Abraham laid his son on the altar was Mt. Moriah. Many generations later, David established his capital in the city that was built on this mount, and on which his son Solomon built the house of the Lord. If so, then the location where Abraham laid his son on an altar may have been very near to or perhaps was right on the spot where centuries later, Jesus would be offered up as a sacrifice.

As God told Abraham He was pleased because he had not withheld his son, his only son, so on Calvary God did not withhold His only Son as a sacrifice for our sins.

Is *that* in the Bible?

Yes – in Genesis 22:1-19 and 2 Chronicles 3:1. The crucifixion account is in all four gospels.

How did Jesus identify his betrayer to the disciples?

The disciples were perplexed as to whom Jesus was referring to when he said that he would soon be betrayed. It didn't matter that Jesus said scripture needed to be fulfilled even when he quoted from the psalms just how the betrayer would be identified, the disciples were still troubled. But not as deeply as their Master was.

Peter motioned to John to ask Jesus who the betrayer was. Jesus answered by citing a custom of his day, in which the host would dip a piece of bread in a bowl and offer it to the guest of honor. This would not have been a strange act to anyone there, nor the apparently appropriate act of offering it to Judas, who was perceived as one of the leaders among the disciples, being the treasurer. (This sign of offering the morsel of bread to Judas must have been explained privately only to John outside the hearing of the other disciples, as implied by the context.) This was the John version.

In the Matthew version, Jesus declared that His betrayer would be he who dipped his hand with him in the bowl. The custom of dipping bread in the same sauce bowl was an act of intimacy and trust.

When Jesus urged Judas to do quickly what he intended to do, some of the disciples thought that Jesus was directing him to handle the financial arrangements for the Passover feast or that he should give some of the money to the poor.

Is *that* in the Bible?

Yes – in Psalm 41:9; Matthew 26:23; Mark 14:10-11, 18; John 13:18-26

[Note - What was the sauce in the bowl? Perhaps sour wine (vinegar) as recorded in Ruth 2:14 when Boaz accorded Ruth a similar courtesy.]

How much did Judas receive to betray Jesus?

Thirty pieces of silver.

Judas was among those who felt in his heart that Jesus as Messiah would surely ascend the throne and overthrow Rome, as was the fervent and mistaken hope of the people. Thus Judas, having seen Jesus perform miracle after miracle, must have felt that Jesus would easily extricate himself from any arrest Judas orchestrated. So he went to the chief priests and asked what they were willing to pay him for delivering Jesus to them. The priests counted out thirty pieces of silver.

When he realized that his expectation wasn't happening and that his plan was going very badly, he sought to return the money and withdraw his betrayal of an innocent man. The Jewish priests would have none of that and so Judas threw down the thirty pieces of silver in the temple, departed and hanged himself.

The chief priests knew that the money, being "the price of blood", wasn't fit to be returned to the treasury so they consulted together and decided to buy the potter's field in which to bury strangers. The field was appropriately named the Field of Blood.

Both the amount of thirty pieces of silver and the potter's field had been prophesied in the Old Testament.

Is _that_ in the Bible?

Yes – in Jeremiah 32:6-9; Zechariah 11:12-13; Matthew 26:14-16; 27:3-10.

In what way was Jesus accursed?

Hanging was not specified as a means of execution in Israel. God commanded that anyone committing a sin deserving of death was to be put to death, then added that if such a person was put to death and the people followed up by hanging the body on a tree, that body was not allowed to remain overnight on the tree but the body was to be buried that day.

God warned that the land that He had given Israel as an inheritance should not be defiled by hanging a body on a tree overnight, "for he who is hanged is accursed of God" or cursed in the sight of God.

Paul used this commandment to draw an analogy to Jesus who hung on the cross to bear the judgment of God upon every sinner. Anyone who is "of the works of the law" is under the curse of the law. In taking upon himself the curse of the Law, Jesus redeemed everyone from that curse, "having become a curse for us (for it is written *'Cursed is everyone who hangs on a tree'*)."

Is _that_ in the Bible?

Yes – in Deuteronomy 21:22-23, Galatians 3:10-13.

How did this accursed symbol acquire an exalted position?

God's love for man was such that He provided a way of escape from the penalty of death even before He created man, knowing ahead of time that man would sin. Jesus would be that sacrificial Lamb slain from the foundation of the world. The instrument of that sacrifice would be a cross on Calvary.

In a magnificent display of His love on such a grand scale, God imprinted His logo of love throughout creation. He adopted the cross, a symbol of shame and degradation on which Jesus was to hang and die, to be his "logo." The design of a cross is embedded in many of nature's plants and designs. For example, in any of the cruciferous (*cross-bearing*) vegetables (broccoli, cauliflower, kale, cabbage), if you slice the stems cross-wise, you will discern a cross in the stem.

One would need to keep his eyes open for God's "Valentine" messages embedded throughout nature for it is the glory of God to conceal a matter.

From the largest to the smallest creations, one can find God's logo. A photograph taken through the Hubble telescope shows a cross in the middle of the M51 spiral galaxy, and an electron microscope photograph of the laminin cell also shows a cross pattern in the cell. Concealed in the laminin cell are symbols of Jesus' redemptive work because the laminin cell functions to hold things together and promote healing of wounds. Jesus is described as existing before anything else, and he holds all creation together. Also, he was wounded by our transgressions, and by his stripes we are healed.

Paul determined to exalt the magnificence of the cross by preaching only Christ and Him crucified.

Is _that_ in the Bible?

Yes – in Proverbs 25:2; Isaiah 53:5; 1 Corinthians 2:2; Colossians 1:17, Revelation 13:8. The Hubble telescope and electron microscope photographs can be viewed by googling *laminin,* which also provides scientific definitions for *laminin.*

What did Peter mean when he said that Pentecost was what Joel had referred to?

The disciples obeyed Jesus' command to tarry for the outpouring of the Holy Spirit before they were to go on the Great Commission. They were all in one place, in one accord, and spent most of the time praying.

Then a series of events happened in succession that was identifiable as manifestations of the Holy Spirit: a sound from heaven as of a rushing mighty wind, divided tongues of fire appearing on top of each head, and speaking in tongues (languages unknown to the speakers but known by others).

People who witnessed this were amazed and perplexed. Many people visiting Jerusalem at that moment recognized these languages being spoken. "Whatever could this mean?" they wondered, and concluded that the disciples were full of new wine.

Peter stood up to explain that they were not drunk for it was only 9 o'clock in the morning, but what the people had just witnessed had been prophesied by the prophet Joel. He then went on to quote the Joel 2 passage. But nowhere in Peter's quoting of the Old Testament prophet were the three manifestations of the Holy Spirit that they had experienced that day mentioned. There was no mention of a sound from heaven, divided tongues of fire, or speaking in tongues.

What Peter was saying was that when the Holy Spirit shows up, one will recognize what's happening even if it isn't specifically described elsewhere or even if it has never happened before.

Is *that* in the Bible?

Yes – in Acts 2 quoting Joel 2:28-32.

Why did Jesus ask Peter "Do you love me?" three times?

Peter had denied his Lord three times, although he had sworn that he would never even leave Him. Succumbing to human nature, he failed where he had boasted he wouldn't fail.

But the events had changed Peter and he sorrowfully humbled himself. Jesus knew this because He could read hearts, but the disciples didn't yet know of Peter's transformation. So as Jesus sought to restore Peter, He asked him three times if Peter loved him.

Just as he had denied his Lord three times, Peter was being given three opportunities to confess his Lord publicly (and be restored to his fellow disciples). Jesus asked "Simon, do you love Me?" (The first time he asked it, he added "more than these" – "Peter, do you love me more than these?" *These* is in the neuter gender, meaning the fish, not Peter's fellow disciples.)

There are two Greek words translated "love" in this passage – *agape* and *phileo*. The first one is unconditional love, a self-giving love that seeks the highest good of the other person without asking anything in return. The second one is a friendship love. Jesus used the *agape* word the first two times that He asked Peter the question, and each time, Peter answered with the *phileo* word.

So the third time, Jesus used the *phileo* word as though to say, "Peter, if that level of love is all you're capable of, then I'm willing to meet you there." And so Jesus asked the same question a third time in a way that Peter could answer honestly.

(Although at the moment, *phileo* was all that Peter had and was capable of giving, he later received the fuller understanding of *agape* love from the Holy Spirit and used the word several times in his epistles.)

Is *that* in the Bible?

Yes – in Mark 14:29-30; John 21:15-17, 1 Peter 1:8, 22; 2:17; 4:8; 2 Peter 1:7.

How much temptation can a person face?

Hardships and tests may come from God for the shaping of our character, but temptations never come from God.

They come from our own desires, which entice us and drag us away and eventually give birth to sinful actions.

Jesus modeled a prayer in which he said "Do not lead us into temptation, but deliver us from the evil one." It is the evil one who tempts us. Jesus was victorious in resisting the enemy three times in the wilderness and those three temptations (lust of the flesh, lust of the eyes, and pride of life) represent all of the temptations to which we are subject today. He was tempted in all points as we are, yet was without sin.

God is faithful who will not allow anyone to be tempted beyond his ability to resist temptation but will with the temptation provide a way of escape. The person who endures temptation is considered blessed and will receive the crown of life that God has promised to those who love him.

How much temptation can a person face? Never more than he is able to endure.

Is *that* in the Bible?

Yes – in Matthew 6:13; 1 Corinthians 10:13; Hebrews 4:15; James 1:12-15; 1 John 2:16.

Was the preservation of Israel's language prophesied?

Language tends to be dynamic and evolves with time and in the context of culture. The older classical Greek language was different from the Greek spoken in Jesus' time (termed *koine* Greek) and since then has metamorphosed to the modern Greek spoken today.

Thus it is startling and nothing short of amazing that a language can be preserved for years and be spoken today essentially the same way it was 2000 years ago. But such is the case with the Hebrew language.

This phenomenon was prophesied in scripture. God said, referring to Israel, "They shall again use this speech in the land of Judah and in its cities, when I bring back their captivity: The Lord bless you, O home of justice, and mountain of holiness!"

Eliezer Ben-Yehuda (1858-1922) learned Hebrew as part of his religious upbringing. Inspired by the Bulgarian, Italian and Greek revivals that brought them back to their native soil, Ben-Yehuda felt that the heirs of historic Jerusalem deserved the same. He determined to do something to emulate those revivals. The Hebrew language to that point was only a written language and not a spoken one, but Ben-Yehuda vowed that he would do something about that. He decided on three main action plans: Hebrew in the Home, Hebrew in the School, and Words, Words, Words.

Even before his family arrived in Palestine, he decided to speak only Hebrew with every Jew he met. Looking forward to a Hebrew-speaking homeland someday, he made his wife Deborah promise to raise their first son, Ben-Zion Ben-Yehuda as the first all-Hebrew speaking child in modern history. Hebrew words were coined for everyday objects. His family became an inspiration for others to emulate. Modeling after the language instruction in Russia where he had been born, Ben-Yehuda waged a campaign to have every rabbi and teacher use Hebrew as the language of instruction in Palestine.

Was *that* prophesied in the Bible?

Yes – in Jeremiah 31:23

Which country will win the Olympics?

The Olympics had been an established Greek tradition and event for seven centuries when Paul wrote several pieces of admonition using metaphors borrowed from the Olympics. The games started in Olympia in 776 B.C. about the time that Homer was born.

The writer of Hebrews uses athletic symbolism by enjoining his readers to lay aside every weight (a reference to the Greek habit of running with weights during an athlete's training and then taking them off for the actual race) and to run with endurance (a reference to marathon races). He also gives this admonition in the setting of an arena such as would be filled with spectators watching the ancient Olympic events ("since we are surrounded by so great a cloud of witnesses").

Paul uses Olympic terms to encourage his readers to run the race, to prepare diligently, and that there is only one prize winner. He wrote Timothy in terms that would be easily understood in the Olympic context – fought, good fight, finished, race, crown.

But while the Bible is a book of prophecies, many already fulfilled and many waiting for fulfillment, it doesn't prognosticate national or individual Olympic event winners. It does provide a profile of those who eventually win: they show diligence in preparation, faithfulness, desire, passion, singlemindedness, focus, self-denial, temperance, discipline, and subjugating the body – all of which are part of the Olympic competitor's experience. And in the context of his admonition that there is only one prize, Paul nevertheless encourages everyone to be a winner.

Is *that* in the Bible?

Yes – all over Proverbs, and in 1 Corinthians 9:24, 27; 2 Timothy 4:7-8; Hebrews 12:1-2.

Who will be the next president?

Although there are instances in which a world leader, such as Cyrus, is identified in advance, the Bible doesn't specifically identify the next president by name. However, we know that the election result won't be by chance or the whim of the people, but by God's will.

It is God who removes kings and raises up kings, who rules in the kingdom of men and gives it to whomever He will. There is no authority except from God, including all communist, despotic or repressive governments, and the authorities that exist are appointed by God.

A biblical requirement for those who rule over men is that they be just and that they rule in the fear of God. Fear here is a response to the awesomeness of God that inspires reverence and respect.

Is *that* in the Bible?

Yes – in 2 Samuel 23:3; 2 Chron. 36:22; Ezra 1:1-8; Daniel 2:21, 4:17. The definition of *fear* is derived from the Hebrew word *morah,* meaning reverence, awe, terror.

How can we decide on election issues?

By holding them up against an uncompromising standard – the Bible.

A political candidate's fitness for office will start with his commitment to a right standard. The righteous leader will be just, ruling in the fear of God, and not swayed by bribes. Wisdom to rule and principles of governance are given throughout scripture. Instruction in righteousness is found in scripture, and the importance of providing that instruction early in life is endorsed. Early instruction in righteousness will help form correct opinions on issues of sanctity of life, welfare, homosexuality, illegal aliens, and social security – all of which are dealt with in scripture.

What a person's makeup and philosophy are is shaped by a lifetime and not by current popular demands. That direction in one's life is given in his diligent pursuit of righteous principles to God's approval, that he may rightly teach and explain the word of truth to others.

When the righteous are in authority, the people rejoice. Citizens are more content and divine favor is poured out on a nation when righteous principles of governance are practiced. This happens when the righteous are in authority.

Is _that_ in the Bible?

Yes – in 2 Samuel 23:3; Proverbs 22:6; 29:2, 4; 2 Timothy 2:15; 3:16.

What should be our responsibility and attitude towards all government?

Exercise your right to vote but once leaders are elected to office, support them as unto the Lord. Remember that He has allowed or chosen them to gain office.

Since there is no authority except from God, including all communist and repressive governments, and the authorities that exist are appointed by God, we are enjoined to be subject to the governing authorities, submitting to man's ordinances for the Lord's sake.

As we contemplate the difficult-to-comprehend situation that this appointment may include despotic governments that persecute God's people and repress the growth of the gospel, we can know that we are given a role in making change. We are admonished to intercede and pray for all who are in authority in order that we may lead peaceable lives.

Such fervent prayer will be effective and avail much and can result in breakthrough in those countries with repressive governments. The reason for our submission to all governments is for the Lord's sake, and this is the will of God. As in all of our responses, we are to do all to the glory of God.

Prayer for the welfare of government and all in authority should come from those who are righteous and upright. When it goes well for these citizens, the city benefits and rejoices. They are the ones who can bless the city, state or national governments.

What a privilege and responsibility we have in determining the outcome of elections by praying the will of God into place. Otherwise, without our prayers, it is possible for the will of God to be delayed. God's purposes can be delayed, as witness the Israelites' 40-year detour in the wilderness.

Is _that_ in the Bible?

Yes – in Numbers 14:29, 34; Proverbs 11:10-11; Jeremiah 29:7; John 19:11, Romans 13:1, 1 Timothy 2:2; Titus 3:1, Hebrews 13:17, James 5:16, 1 Peter 2:13-17.

What did the white stone mean?

The person who overcomes is promised a white stone and written on it a new name. Jacob was a deceiver but overcame his past and received a new name, because names have meanings and a change of names can reflect a change of character or destiny.

(Thus Abram became Abraham, Sarai became Sarah, Jacob became Israel, Simon became Peter and Saul became Paul.)

So what did the white stone, on which the new name was to be written, signify?

In the jury system of the day, a stone was cast in an urn as a vote – black for guilty and white for acquittal. Paul referred to this practice when, accused by the Jews, he spoke in his defense before King Agrippa. He recounted his experience in chasing down Christians and helping to condemn them to death by casting his vote against them. That vote would have been the casting of a black stone.

Is _that_ in the Bible?

Yes – in Acts 26:10; Revelation 2:17. The jury system of the day as described above is historical.

Who was Mammon?

Most people think 'mammon' means money. Not quite.

Mammon stands for money because Mammon was the Philistine god of money. The comparison between mammon and God was intended to elicit worship of the true God and not to serve idols and other gods, the most prominent of which is mentioned here as mammon.

Money is occasionally called the root of all evil, misquoting the passage by omitting the words "the love of" in front of "money." Money management is a God-given gift. If you're gifted at managing money, would you be serving Mammon? Not necessarily.

The reference to mammon in scripture was in the context of lordship and does not exclude the stewardship of money as one of our gifts and responsibilities. The admonition is that one cannot serve God and any other idol at the same time, the example given being the idol of money. An idol is anything that comes between our worship of God and God. The clear admonition is that we cannot serve God unless we serve only Him.

Is _that_ in the Bible?

Yes – in Matthew 6:24; Luke 16:13, 1 Timothy 6:10

Who is the elect lady and her children?
Dirarsen Lovas

The apostle John addressed his second epistle to "the elect lady and her children." Who was this woman?

Some think it could have been a hospitable Christian woman whose children persevered in the faith, as indicated in verse 4. There even is reference to greetings from her nieces and nephews later in the epistle.

Others think that the woman is symbolic of a church, consistent with imagery in other parts of Scripture. That would make "her children" members of that church and the nieces and nephews children of her "elect sister" the members of another church, likely the local one from which John wrote his letter.

There is no strong consensus regarding which view is the right one.

Is *that* in the Bible?

Yes – in 2 John

Who was Jude?

Sujita Adhakari

Jude, one of the shortest Bible books at one chapter of 25 verses, is the second to the last book in the Bible, just before Revelation. It is a letter warning an unknown community of Christians against false teachers. Names of books that are letters usually carried the names of either the ones addressed (like Timothy, Thessalonians, Corinthians, Titus, Philemon) or the name of the letter writer. In this case, Jude is the author of the book bearing his name.

He identifies himself as the brother of James, most likely the James who was the brother of Jesus and leader of the Jerusalem church. Mark 6:3 mentions Judas as a brother of the Lord, and with Jude's claim in verse 1, this Jude would be the Judas whom Mark mentions as being Jesus' brother.

Is *that* in the Bible?

Yes – in Mark 6:3, Jude

Why did Jesus cry "It is finished"?

The gospels record 7 last words or statements that Jesus uttered from the cross. The last one was a commitment of his spirit to his Father just before he died. But preceding that was a loud and triumphant cry, "It is finished."

What was finished?

Jesus lived a sinless life, resisting and overcoming all of the enemy's temptations, and presented a perfect, spotless sacrifice on the cross to pay for mankind's sins. By atoning for our sins, Jesus brought us back into right standing with the Father as though we had never sinned. It was for this purpose that Jesus came and lived a sinless life in perfect obedience to his Father's will. It was in exultant triumph that he declared the conflict won.

The enemy had lost.

The work of redemption was complete. (The tense of the original language means that this act of completion was done once and for all time and its results would abide continuously.)

The work was finished.

The victory was obtained.

Praise the Lord for we are the beneficiary of that victory!

Is _that_ in the Bible?

Yes – in John 19:30.

CONJECTURES

This section considers some possibilities that don't have as solid a scripture basis as required, but may still be of reader interest. Some of these may someday find archaeological support and be moved to the first section; or they may languish here for insufficient historical or scholarly support. They nevertheless remain interesting points.

What is the eye of the needle?

In the United States, some homes have a small opening at the bottom of their back doors with a swinging cover, to allow house pets easy access and exit. In Israel today, some homes have a similar door within a door but much larger than those in the United States. They take up the lower half of the regular-size door. Tour guides like to point them out as the "eye of the needle" that Jesus referred to.

If so, the hyperbole is still preserved as a device which Jesus effectively used to drive home his point, but a fresh application is revealed. Through such a large eye of the needle, it is still possible for a camel to go but it would first have to be divested of any load on its back, and it must get down on its knees. Even then, it would be with extreme difficulty to have it pass through this opening.

Is _that_ in the Bible?

Yes – the term is used in Matthew 19:24 and Luke 18:25, but not identified specifically as a door within a door except in modern-day Israel.

Was King Tut the Pharaoh's first-born son who was killed by the angel of death?

Perhaps, perhaps not.

It took years for any king to have a tomb built. Many times it took his lifetime or longer. That the young Tut would have such a colossal tomb ready might be ascribed to the possibility that it was his father's. When the pharaoh drowned in the Red Sea in pursuit of the Israelites, it would have been a logical step to bury his dead first-born son in an already-made tomb. (Dating the exodus to correspond with King Tut's place in the Egyptian dynasty would also remain a challenge.)

References: Exodus 12:12, 29.

Did John the Baptist really eat locusts?

Yes, but perhaps not the crawling, flying type.

The locust was a clean animal and conceivably could have been part of John the Baptist's diet. But *locust* was also a term used to identify the carob tree and its edible fruit. Given that John the Baptist was a lifelong Nazirite, it is highly likely that the locusts he ate in the desert were the fruiting kind, not the flying kind.

References: Leviticus 11:21-22, Matthew 3:4; Mark 1:6.

What grave is revered by Muslims, Jews, and Christians alike?

No one's grave has the acknowledgement of all three major religions as Job's does. Abraham would have received the same respect but his grave in the cave of Machpelah before Mamre, which he had bought from Ephron the Hittite, is unmarked.

(Before he died in Egypt, Jacob asked that he be buried in this same cave in which his grandfather Abraham and grandmother Sarah were buried, and in which he buried his father Isaac and wife Leah.)

Job's grave is in southern Arabia. Job was a historical figure whose life story was the subject of the first written book of the Bible.

Is _that_ in the Bible?

Yes – in Genesis 23; 25:8-9; 49:29-33. Job's grave site in Southern Arabia, traditionally acknowledged by all three religions, is not specifically identified in the Bible.

Was Jonah really swallowed by a whale?

Scholars say "not likely" and quote science as their basis.

The Bible says that God prepared a large fish to swallow Jonah. We then assume that this fish must have been a whale but marine biologists point out that no whale is capable of opening its throat wide enough to swallow a man. Whales would choke on even a small fish if swallowed whole. Their diet consists of plankton and small to large fish which are chewed first into small bits before being swallowed.

But if not a whale, which fish could have swallowed Jonah? That would be anybody's guess but we should not rule out the whale – and we have good reason to believe it was because God was in control of the situation. "He had prepared" indicates that God was orchestrating the whole event. He can do anything – even open up the whale's throat, preserving Jonah alive in a closed environment that would otherwise rob him of oxygen, and finally having the whale disgorge Jonah unharmed.

The narrative states "So the Lord spoke to the fish and it vomited Jonah onto dry land." God was in charge all the way. So couldn't He prescribe a whale's modification to accommodate the circumstances? Yes, of course, for He is God to whom nothing is impossible.

References: Jeremiah 32:17, 27; Jonah 1-2.

Is it true that the redeemed will have as many stars in their crown as souls they have won?

There was a popular gospel song of another generation whose title was "Will there be any stars in my crown?" It may have been responsible for, or the result of, a belief that the redeemed will have in their crowns as many stars, or gemstones, as souls whose salvation they were directly responsible for by their witness.

There is no biblical support for this.

What there is, is support for gemstones in Jesus' crown representing the redeemed. God characterized His people in Zechariah 9:16 as being like jewels of a crown though used in the context of spiritual warfare. It would be more appropriate that we, as trophies of the cross, become jewels in Jesus' crown.

A more accurate gospel song reflects this alternate view in its first stanza and refrain –

When He cometh, when He cometh to make up His
    jewels,
All His jewels, precious jewels, His loved and His own.
Like the stars of the morning, His bright crown
adorning,
They shall shine in their beauty, bright gems for His
    crown,

reflecting Malachi 3:17 – "They shall be Mine," says the Lord of hosts, "on the day that I make them My jewels...."

Why did the purification rites take seven days?
Leni Puen

When Miriam and Aaron spoke out against Moses because of the Ethiopian woman he had married, God summoned all three to the tabernacle of meeting. He reaffirmed His servant Moses before Miriam and Aaron but His anger was aroused against them and He departed.

Suddenly Miriam was as white as snow with leprosy. Aaron, who as priest had to deal with leprosy in his duties and understood the severity of the situation, pleaded with Moses to intercede for her. God directed that she be shut out of the camp for seven days, bringing the whole forward progress of the Israelites to a halt while they awaited the end of Miriam's isolation.

The reference to this period and process of purification goes back to God's instructions to the priests for ceremonial cleansing of anyone healed of a serious skin disease. Part of it was that the person had to be isolated outside the camp for seven days.

Why seven?

We aren't told specifically in scripture, but numbers and other details provided were never arbitrary. (For example, the many rules of what we now define as personal or community hygiene were enforced, though without scientific explanation provided then, for the good and the health of the community. God had instructed His people through Moses to not act like the people in Egypt or Canaan to imitate their way of life, "for I am the Lord your God." By obeying all His regulations and decrees, He assured them, they would find life through them.)

Since seven days were specified in this purification process, isn't it interesting to conjecture that there might be some connection to today's medical practice wherein doctors specify that any antibiotic series prescribed be taken for seven consecutive days?

As there is nothing incidental in scripture and we only need time to have science validate the correctness of practices God directed Israel to observe, perhaps we may find a connection between the seven of the purification period and the seven of the antibiotic series.

Is _that_ in the Bible?

Yes – The purification rites are, in Leviticus 14:2-9; 18:2-5; Numbers 12:1-15.

When the disciples cast the net on their boat's right side at Jesus' command, why was the number of fish caught 153?

The disciples had toiled all night fishing with not a single catch. In the wee hours of the morning, Jesus appeared and called out from the beach asking if they had any food (any catch). When they said no, He said "Cast the net on the right side of the boat and you will find some."

The result was a great catch and Peter dragged the net to land. Yet though it was full of large fish, the net was not broken. The total catch was 153 fish.

Is _that_ in the Bible?

Yes – the story is found in John 21:1-

Perhaps the number 153 doesn't mean anything but nothing included in scripture is insignificant. A marine biologist has suggested that there are 153 families of fish in the world. Could it be that Jesus was saying that we are to fish for and bring in all the families of the world? And that if we do, the net (methods) we use for catching them will not fail? We cannot strain any net enough – whether by radio, TV, satellite, internet, public evangelism or personal witness – to bring in the catch for the kingdom.

One more point: because Jesus had directed them to cast their net on the right side, they must be presumed to have been fishing off the left side of the boat towards the deep. Thus it is significant that they got their catch when they cast their net towards shore. The right side of the boat would have faced Jesus. Also, Jesus' side is always the "right" side.

The following readers contributed Questions used in this Edition.

Aanand Limbu

Adwin (Ace) Apostol

Amos Sinchuri

Anjaan Shrestha

Asyll Saberola

Bodem D. Koh

Benjamin Banaag

Bojo Lijauco

Carmi Flores

Charles Danuwar

Charlow Dedicatoria

Dake M. Deere

Dawa Lama

Debora Munnu Rai

Dipak Upreti

Dirarsen Lovas

Donald Esguerra

Edison Apostol

Ernie Banaag

Evonne Williams

Ferry Rosos

Flor D. Bayurla

Gard R. Wymalife

Garry B. Mupas

Genalin Lopez

Generis L. Avafada

Gener Samboy Quiambao

Giddell Garcia

Gideon N. Urarte

Gloria (Oyie) Banaag

Gloria (Gigi) Guzman

Gloria Williams

Glory N. Ersola

Glory S. Nytogaard

Grace A. Mason

Grayce Sarmiento

Gregg S. L. Ovalime

Homer Mendoza

Jessica Jalober

Jismar Abquilan

John Bayalkoti

John D. Deeke

John Jena

John Christopher Puen

Joseph Quiambao

Khongkrit Inkamon

Leni B. Puen

Leizl Joy Briza

Letty Banaag

Letty Protacio

Lota Apostol

Lou Vincent May

Lozala Ferrer

M. Pedro Cigras

Mahendra Thapa

Marco Leon

Marie Aleli C. Haboc

Mark DiMaggio

Marven Adap

Mehl Dizon

Melissa Tanap

Michelle Yanez

Mickie Hall

Miguel Ferrusquia

Migurawanak Ven Disauranjok

Migy T. Reswand

Mikal Thapa

Nellie Rizo

Peter Boro

Peter L. Giespy

Prabina Manandhar

Preyapone Pumturn

Priscilla Shrestha

Rachel Pariyar

Rebekah Shrestha

Redeem Ebora

Rendex Hart

Ruth Pradhan

Sam Young

Satis Thapa

Satya Majhi

Stacy Gorgone

Stephen Shrestha

Sujita Adhakari

Synthia Webster

Tom Hamilton

Vancine Wilson

Viroj Siriwatanakamol

Zeny B. Mupas

Zernan Diaz

Is _That_ in the Bible?

Do you have a Bible question you would like to see published? In response to this invitation in the first edition, a few readers submitted some questions which we've used for this edition. You will see their italicized names under the questions they submitted. If you have a question you would like to contribute and it is used in a future edition, you will receive printed credit and a copy of the book. Please email questions to rpuen@yahoo.com

To receive similar Bible questions and answers every week, request the Daily Quiz at rpuen@yahoo.com. These are based on the daily reading of the One Year Bible.

Caseloads of this book may be received free of charge by small- to mid-size churches interested in embarking on house church planting or the formation of Bible study groups. For details, contact the author at rpuen@yahoo.com.

CPSIA information can be obtained
at www.ICGtesting.com
Printed in the USA
BVHW070105050222
627844BV00003B/64